The Bramley

An Anthology of Flash Fiction Armagh

Edited by Byddi Lee and in Irish by Réamonn Ó Ciaráin

Individual Pieces © Respective Authors, 2019

Sliocht as *'Cití na gCártaí'* Réaltán Ní Leannáin, *Cití na gCártaí* (Cois Life, 2019).
ISBN: 978-1-907494-93-2 © Réaltán Ní Leannáin & Cois Life, Foilsithe le caoinchead Cois Life
Excerpt from /Sliocht as *'Dílis'* le Réaltán Ní Leannáin, Cló Iar-Chonnacht (2015)

L'Origine du Monde Speaks by P.V. Wolseley was first published by *Flash Frontier* in 2014

The Power of A Peeler by Trish Bennet - Previously published: Mar 2018, Recorded by Lisburn 98 FM for Lisburn Reads. Nov 2016, *The Leitrim Guardian* 2017. July 2016, BBC Radio Ulster Time of Our Lives. June 2013, *Ireland's Own*.

After the Conflict by Peter Hollywood is from the collection *Hawks and Other Short Stories* published by New Island Books.

The Boy Corps of Eamhain Mhacha by Réamonn Ó Ciaráin is a section from *Cúchulainn – Ulster's Greatest Hero* by Réamonn Ó Ciaráin, published by Gael Linn www.gael-linn.ie
Lugh ag Teacht i gCabhair ar Chúchulainn, Glacadh Arm & an Chéad Mharú, Bás Chúchulainn le Réamonn Ó Ciaráin from *Laoch na Laochra - Scéal Chúchulainn* (2015) Gael Linn www.gael-linn.ie

Box Room by Maureen Boyle was previously published in *Happy Browsing - An Anthology in Praise of Bookfinder'*, published by *The Tangerine* in 2018.

Incunabula III by Maureen Boyle is from *The Work of a Winter* published 2018 by Arlen House Press.

Kilty Relics was awarded 'The Leitrim Guardian Literary Award for Poetry' and published in its 2018 edition.

Revisiting by Elaine Toal was first published in *Circling Round Conformity*, published in 2018 by Dunfanaghy Writers' Circle and edited by Alf McCreary.

The Realisation by Jude Alexzander was published in *The Blue Nib* magazine in December 2019.

Keady Graveyard Sunday by Damien Mallon was previously published in *Reading the Trees* by Damien Mallon.

Hurricane Glamping by Elaine Toal was first published in *Circling Round Conformity*, published in 2018 by Dunfanaghy Writers' Circle and edited by Alf McCreary.

Tá *Scáile Dheirdre* sa chnuasacht gearrscéalta Go mBeinnse Choíche Saor le Máire Dinny Wren a d'fhoilsigh Éabhlóid in 2016.

Reading the Trees by Damien Mallon was previously published in Reading the Trees by Damien Mallon

The Joke by Csilla Toldy first appeared in The Emigrant Woman's Tale Lapwing Publications (2015) ISBN 978-1909252998 [book and CD]

ISBN: 9781794429253

CONTENTS

ACKNOWLEDGMENTS

Thanks are due to the wonderful Karen Mooney for planting the apple seed that grew into the Bramley while having a conversation with her about how we could compensate the superb writers who read at the Flash Fiction Armagh events. She suggested publishing the stories in a journal and here we are!

Flash Fiction Armagh would never have gotten off the ground had it not been for the courageous indulgence of the award-winning Mulberry Bistro in Armagh. They allowed us to experiment with the event in their beautiful upstairs room, which we now think of as the home grounds for Flash Fiction Armagh.

We are also grateful for the support we've received from Armagh City, Banbridge and Craigavon Borough Council who have encouraged us to participate in the wonderful festivals held throughout Armagh during the year. We had a wonderful evening at the Armagh Cider Company during the Food and Cider Festival in September.

Special thanks to the Armagh County Museum for hosting us in January 2019 and for their generous donation towards this publication.

We are grateful to every writer who submits to Flash Fiction Armagh. We are honoured to read your work.

Thank you to the people who attend the events.

Together, you make the magic that we now call Flash Fiction Armagh!

Go raibh maith agat.

Wake Up Call

Cathy Carson

Did I mention that I love my baby?
God, I just love the weight of him, I love the smell of him, the way
the light catches the down on his skin.
I adore the way his toes curl when he giggles.
My favourite part of the day is bath time when the soft give in the
flesh feels like bread dough beneath my fingers and his long lashes sit
plump with water against his cheeks.
But sometimes.
Like now.
In this moment.
When that constant screaming assaults my senses, jangles my
nerves… I don't think I love him at all.
Sometimes, I imagine grabbing him by the shoulders and shaking
him.
Hard!
I press the tiny body, red with rage into the cot with more force than
is needed and back out of the room.
Easing closed the bathroom door, I slide down the cool tiles until I'm
sat on the floor.
Christ!
I can still bloody hear him!
I draw my knees up, lace my fingers through my hair and tug with all
my strength.
The pain is bliss.
It is just good to feel something other than resentment, something
other than failure.
I let the tears fall fast, my own gulping sobs drowning out the
screaming.

My body is aching from lack of sleep and there is a constant nausea that gnaws at my gut.

I am not meant to be a mother.

I know that now.

Christ, I know it in every inch of my skin.

There is silence.

Has he actually stopped?

Relief floods me as the promise of sleep beckons.

As I pass the cot, I check him.

Something is wrong.

Something is very wrong.

His legs are rigid, fists clenched and he is trembling.

Eyes wide, cheeks flushed and he isn't making a sound.

He doesn't even see me.

I reach out to touch him and his skin is blazing.

I start to pray.

I can't remember the last time I prayed.

But right now I would make a deal with the devil if he was standing in front of me.

I think God answers.

Because even though my blood is puddling in my feet and my skin feels like it is shrinking, I manage to pick up my phone and call for help.

And somehow from a call centre somewhere, a lady called Janice takes control of my hands and I find myself removing his clothing and his nappy and placing him on his side.

She asks me how long he has been like this.

I am sick with shame because I don't know the answer.

But she tells me to count the time from now and that help is on its way.

At fifty-six seconds, it stops.

Tiny fists unfurl into stars.

Legs that were rigid begin to wriggle and kick.

And then he screams.

It is the most precious sound.

I let the notes of it wash over me, washing me clean washing away all that has gone before.

I pick him up and place his damp cheek against my neck.

God, I just love the weight of him, I love the smell of him.
I breathe him in.
He is mine.
And I am meant to be his mother.

Always and Forever

Jay Faulkner

She's at the door. Still.

I don't need to look, down from our bedroom window, the full moon illuminating her in too bright detail, to see her.

I know she's there.

She's been there for the last three days. The last three nights.

Nights are the worst. It's then I miss her most. In the two years we'd been married, we'd never slept apart. The same ritual, from our first night together to our last: undress each other, climb between the cold sheets and warm each other as we made love. Then, finally, we'd lie face to face, whispering our personal mantra before falling asleep:

'I love you.'

'I love you, too.'

'Always.'

'Forever.'

She's at the door. Again. I don't need to look. She's been there ever since she died.

When it began experts said it was just a variation of seasonal flu. Two weeks later hospitals were overflowing and the military had been deployed to quell riots in major cities. The flu outbreak became an epidemic so fast it overwhelmed the country. The epidemic turned into an apocalypse; at least according to the last radio transmissions we'd heard. The voice on the radio never said where he was, but when he wasn't quoting from the Bible, or quietly sobbing to himself, he was repeating the same information over and over.

The dead walked.

When I first heard him say that, I thought maybe he was infected; perhaps insanity or delusion was one of the symptoms. But his story didn't change. For two days he reported that the dead were moving, attacking healthy people, and tearing them apart.

Devouring them.

We didn't believe it, at first. Then the power died, the phones too, finally, even the radio went quiet. And we were afraid.

Rebecca and I didn't make love that night. The sheets never warmed beneath us. We just held each other, our bodies forming a sanctuary around her swollen stomach as if we could protect our unborn child with ourselves. Six months earlier we'd cried at the news that we'd finally created life, and now, in the cold, dark night, we cried again.

I hoped that, living in the middle of nowhere on our old farm, we'd be safe from the outbreak and the horrors it brought. We were miles and hours away from the nearest city. We *would* be safe.

But the next day Rebecca was sick. We both smiled thin smiles and pretended it was just a morning sickness. She hadn't been sick throughout the whole pregnancy but maybe she had a price to pay for becoming a mother after all. When a swelling under her armpit started to bleed, and a fever set in, we stopped smiling.

I sat with her all that day and through the night. I mopped her scarlet skin with tepid water and wiped vomit from her mouth. She cried red tears through swollen eyes, and screamed in pain-fuelled incoherency.

And then she stilled.

I rested my hand on her stomach and prayed. I watched her chest rise and fall, slow and gentle. Exhausted, I leaned my head against her head, ignoring the smell of sickness...

...sunlight pierced my eyes as I woke in a silent bedroom. The sweat stained sheets were empty. As I staggered to my feet, I caught my reflection in the dresser mirror and the words scrawled there in her favorite lipstick.

'...always.'

I stumbled down the stairs and heard a rhythmic thumping coming from beyond the kitchen. I ran through fallen chairs and scattered tablecloth then saw her through the window in the door. Her skin taut and pale, eyes fixed and glassy, she walked into the door time, after time, after time.

I fell to my knees and swallowed the bitter taste of bile. As I'd slept in our bed, that final night together, she'd used the last of her strength to stagger from the house, our house, and die alone in the night. She'd known what she would become, what she would've done to me, if she'd died in my arms.

Now I've been sitting in our bedroom, alone, for three days and three nights, listening as she walks into the door, trying to return home. Return to me.

Enough.

I walk down to the kitchen where moonlight streams in through the glass. I open the door. She moves toward me with a rictus smile of...longing? I see her swollen stomach writhe and my eyes fill.

I wait for her embrace with a whisper of: 'Forever ...'

Feidhmiú an Ranga (Classroom Operations)

Seán Ó Farraigh

They judge me
in the blink of an eye,
bheadh siad do mo cheistiú
go dtí deireadh Mhí Iúil.

They scrutinise my appearance
on a daily basis,
's iad ag pleidhcíocht thart
a bhíonn do mo chrá!

I give out a plethora of instructions
but alas, they fall on deaf ears,
bím ag amharc i dtreo an chloig go minic
"in ainm Dé, nach bhfuil an lá seo an-fhada!"

I am asked the same question repeatedly
regardless of the time,
"A mhúinteoir, an bhfuil cead agam dul chuig an leithreas?"
déanta na fírinne, ní heol dom cad chuige nach bhfuil mé faoi chré!

Neverthelss their attention is transformed when stars are mentioned
and their zeal becomes palpable,
's nuair a ghlactar le mo chomhairle gan smaoineamh uirthi
cuireann sé drithlíní faitís le mo dhroim!

I have spent more than three months
with this Primary three class,
's cé go raibh mé thuas seal, thíos seal leo
is cinnte nach ndéanfaidh mé dearmad orthu go deo!

Hope

Jude Alexzander

It was hard to believe that Peter would be six by now. Two whole years had passed – years of endless phone calls, form-filling and retelling her story. Of going around and around in circles under the soulless fluorescent lights and the blandly sympathetic looks that said *'Oh, my God. Oh, you poor, poor woman. Oh, I'm so glad this is not happening to me.'*

Twenty four months of fruitless searching, up and down the country, boxes of flyers bumping around in the car amongst the debris of her life. The posters seemed to mock her – hundreds of lifeless images of his laughing face looking back at her from the passenger seat. The seat where he should have been sitting.

Sigrid's eyes stung as she stared down at the crumpled piece of paper. Two years, three investigators and every penny of her savings – all distilled down into two little words and a foreign phone number, scrawled out furtively on a dirty scrap. Hope was so fragile. If someone answered, what would she say? Would she even hear them over the pounding of her own heartbeat? And if they didn't- what then?

The worn plastic phone sat on the desk, cord curled innocently around it, like the tail of a sleeping dragon. Time seemed to stretch out impossibly as she dialled with shaking fingers and listened to the hollow silence on the line. Then suddenly – click. A polished, polite voice rang in her ear, and her stomach sank.

'The number you have dialled is out of service. Please check the number, and try again.'

She replaced the receiver gently, staring at it unseeing as the numbness settled over her once more. Hope is such a fragile thing.

Twist or pull?

Sue Divin

Predictable as sunshine on the Twelfth that I'd get spied. I'd shimmied up the tree with all the prowess of incy-wincy-spider. Now, frozen to the branch, I was regretting the brightness of my Armagh Gaelic shirt. It hadn't been Mr O'Hagan I'd been hoping to see over the orchard wall but then again, I hadn't taken him for the type to be oogling Judge Judy of a morning neither.

'Toul' ye tay wear green,' Mark hissed up at me, jiggling our loot in his sister's schoolbag.

I'd blend in by the end of Autumn at the rate I was edging along the final branch. Cheek of him - slagging me when he'd a pink Barbie rucksack bustin' with Bramleys.

'Sure I'd nothing green,' I whispered back.

'Some Irishman you.' He winked.

After seven years at integrated primary together, I could let him away with it. Almost. Stretching, I yanked the next apple and fired it at him. 'There's an orange for ye – case you're feeling left out.'

'Twist, don't pull!' he yelped in a voice that was still showing no sign of breaking.

The google-guru knew everything about cider home-brewing, except how to climb the bloody tree. Twist was, from my vantage point, this *was* all about pulling. I'd a cracker view into Grainne O'Hagan's back garden. Her knickers on the line were flying in glorious technicolour and it would take more than the fizz of an illicit pint behind Mark's shed to cool me down. Truth be told, a few litre bottles of cider would be easier come by through the bribing of my cousin, for he had a fake ID and a quare shadow of a beard but sure, where would you be without a bit of dare? Odds on, not monkeying in a flippin' tree. If I didn't get a move on, the verdict wouldn't just be dished out from Judge Judy - Grainne's Da was shifting in his chair.

'That enough yet?' I asked.

'One more,' says he, pointing like the executioner.

It's a real beauty, just out of reach - story of my life. I'm stretching now like a turn of my wrist will reveal super-power finger extensions, the heady combination of the honey orchard air and the rainbow of underwear fuelling my self-belief. Course I can reach this. I can. Just...

Crack.

Shite.

I'm testing Einstein's theory without the bloody apple. Or was it Newton?

Thwack.

Buzzing in my head.

Blackness.

***

A different buzzing. My brain slowly tunes into the bees and the birds, birds and the bees. There's slabber round my mouth. My hand is being stroked. 'Grainne?' I mumble. My wrist is dropped quicker than a fart in the school corridor. My eyes focus as I lurch upright.

'Mark?'

We stare like pistols at dawn.

'You... you could've been dying,' says he, scuffling away from me in the grass.

It might be believable were it not for his sudden interest in picking daisies. That and the fact he looks like he'd rather be pushing them up. I swallow, wiping my mouth on my T-shirt. *God.* They hadn't covered this one in PSE class. All and well, they made sure we were drilled to know orchards were rife with forbidden fruit but in religion class it was always girls doing the tempting and with that, I was sweet.

As I rub my head, Mark jumps to his feet, apples flooding from the pink rucksack as he flees through the trees. At the far hedge, he looks back once, tears streaming.

***

My stomach was rumbling by the time I found him, down by the shuck, firing stones.

'I'm dead. Am't I?' says he, without looking at me.

He was right and all. Never mind his school rugby squad, his Da would take to it like a duck to slurry. On the positive though, at least he wouldn't be fighting me to sneak a coke-bottle of cider to Grainne. I breathed deep. 'Look, how you ice your cake is your own business,' says I after a minute, 'but you're still the one that knows how to make cider and I reckon you and me both could use a drink.'

Gardener's World

Anne McMaster

On a soft, late spring evening, with dusk spanielled at His heels, God moved slowly through the garden, easing His tired muscles that were now hot and close and tight from a long day's work. He stretched slowly and luxuriantly as He walked; contented, now, that the framework for the early garden was taking shape and His long day's work was almost done.

Eden was looking well tonight, He thought; He'd carefully followed the gardening magazines' recommendations on how to prepare the plots over the winter - a bit of an irony there (He smiled to Himself) as He'd created the humans He now looked to for advice - but their knowledge had paid dividends. Already, the garden showed promise. Raised beds were filled and ready, plants were pruned and even the skeletal fruit canes stood patiently to attention, ready for the growing sun. God paused and, with a quiet smile, visualised the various parts of Eden, later in the year, when they would blossom fresh and luxuriantly green - bearing a myriad of leaves and tiny buds promising heavy crops of salads, vegetables and sweet-jewelled fruits.

The long hedge at the back was freshly mulched - and roses (His favourite flower – if God could admit to being partial) would shortly offer Him their scented blossoms – their delicate scents rising, heady and warm in His cupped palm. Weeds had been lifted, butts filled and paths scoured. Yes, the old place was looking well, He thought, easing His corporeal form carefully onto His spade as He leaned into the soil and looked across the gently undulating land.

In the corner, by the spare plant pots, the organic compost heap, the wormery and the random tools stored carefully in sharp sand, an evening bonfire glowed – thickly glistening orange tongues of flame licking hungrily at the twigs and branches God had carefully pruned. What a boon, He thought, today; what a blessing and a boon.

To find, out in that distant corner of the garden, when He needed it most, that coruscating heap of sputtering flame. Deep within its golden coals, yes, there remained the odd singed feather or a now heat-dulled jewel. But the smell of burning angel would pass – eventually – and every busy gardener (the Almighty smiled to Himself at the serendipity) needs a bonfire, after all…

Cool Customer

Mairead Breen

I glanced towards the door of the café just as she came through, and was captivated. It was her coat that first caught my eye, a knee-length, mohair-type, lime green coat. She refreshed the café, profusely decorated in orange and black for Halloween, as she strode confidently to the counter and placed an order.

Below the hem of her coat, a fine black net hung down to her calf. Underneath the net black leggings stopped above a bare ankle outlining shapely but broader legs than I would have expected for a woman of her seemingly slim build. She could have been a dancer, I thought. Her purple patent, crocodile-skin moccasins contrasted beautifully with the rest of her outfit, betraying an enviable flair for style and colour.

Her flawless skin seemed very pale under short spiky hair that at first looked black, like her expertly-applied, but rather heavy, eye and eyebrow makeup. As she stepped back into the light of the window I saw that her hair wasn't black at all but a dark plum colour. Certainly not natural, I decided.

Her easy familiarity with the counter staff said that she'd been here before. She might have been a local – I wouldn't know. After waiting with graceful patience for an order that seemed to want to hold her there, she slowly picked coins from a small pink purse to hand across the counter. She glided to the door and as she closed it the colours of Halloween filled and dimmed the room once more.

Watching her leave and get into a large black car parked across the street, I realized that while she'd been in the café her vehicle had completely blocked the closed security gates of the car park of the apartment building opposite. A large NO PARKING sign with a warning about penalties was prominently displayed on one of the gates. I wondered at her audacity but with her kind of cool, you could probably expect to get away with just about anything.

Sliocht as 'Cití na gCártaí'

Réaltán Ní Leannáin

Bhuail athair Kati, Ġanni di Felici, leo de thaisme. Bhí an bheirt saighdiúirí tuirseach i ndiaidh cuairt a thabhairt ar na séipéil agus ar na heaglaisí ar fad, ag déanamh iontais den tsaibhreas iontu – marmar, ór agus airgead – agus ag lasadh coinnle nó dhó anseo is ansiúd. Faoi ardtráthnóna bhí siad ag cuartú dí. Shiúil siad suas síos caolsráideanna Mdina ar lorg teach tábhairne, ach turas in aisce a bhí acu. Sa deireadh rinne siad ar an gheata snoite agus amach leo thar an mhóta chuig Rabat, an baile ba ghaire dóibh. Cé go raibh Rabat níos nua-aimseartha mar bhaile bhí a cuid sráideanna lán chomh cúng le sráideanna Mdina. Shiúil an bheirt acu idir na tithe arda ar achan taobh, ach níorbh fhada gur stad siad. D'éist siad. Chuala siad ceol agus gáire agus cling gloiní. D'amharc siad ar a chéile agus tháinig aoibh ar a n-aghaidh. Rinne siad ar dhoras tí a bhí ar oscailt agus shiúil siad isteach go faiteach.

Siopa fíona a bhí ann, é dorcha agus fionnuar istigh. Ní raibh de throscán san áit ach cuntar fada ar chúl an tí le go leagfaí gloiní air, agus binse taobh le balla amháin le go suífeadh seanfhondúirí an bhaile air. Bhí roinnt fear áitiúil ón áit ann, iad i ndiaidh teacht abhaile ó na páirceanna, deannach na ngort ar a gcuid éadaigh, ag ól agus ag gabháil cheoil thuas ag an chuntar.

'Dia sa teach,' arsa Tomaí agus Páidí as béal a chéile.

*

Chuala Kati an scéal óna hathair an lá dar gcionn, i ndiaidh am dinnéir. Bhí Ziju Manwel ag an tábla chomh maith. Bhí an chlann ar fad cruinnithe thart ar an tábla mhór adhmaid sa phríomhsheomra: Ġanni, Ziju Manwel, an ceathrar cailíní, Zija Ġiġi, agus seanmháthair na gcailíní, Nanna.

Bhí na comhlaí druidte ar an fhuinneog bheag a thug amach ar an tsráid, agus na lampaí ola lasta. Bhí an áit geal go leor, nó bhí solas á fhrithchaitheamh thart ar an tseomra ag na ballaí bána aolchloiche. Bhí drisiúr taobh le balla amháin agus bhí na crúiscíní agus na gloiní uilig istigh ann ag glioscarnach go meidhreach faoi loinnir na lampaí.

Ní raibh fágtha den dinnéar ach grabhróga den bhuilbhín eorna, agus roinnt glasraí.

'Tóg an fuílleach bia sin suas staighre, a Vanna agus a Marta,' arsa Nanna.

Bhí Marta réidh le gearán a dhéanamh, nó bhíodh an jab sin ag Vanna amháin de ghnáth. Ach bhíodh eagla ar Vanna dul in airde ar an díon léi féin i ndorchacht na hoíche. D'fhan Marta ina tost agus chuaigh sí féin agus Vanna in airde staighre leis an fhuílleach.

Nuair a d'fhill siad bhí a n-athair is a n-uncail in ard-ghiúmar, ag ól gloine *limoncello* agus ag ríomh scéal na hoíche roimhe.

'Thit achan duine san áit ina thost. Sheas siadsan ag an chuntar agus d'ordaigh siad deoch. Ní minic a thagann na Sasanaigh isteach inár siopaí fíona, ná níl muid ag iarraidh iad a fheiceáil iontu ach oiread. Sheas muid féin inár staic, ag stánadh orthu.'

Lig Manwel gáire mór agus lean seisean leis an scéal.

'Shíl siad nach raibh Béarla ar bith againn, agus níor lig muid orainn go raibh. Dúirt duine amháin acu leis an duine eile, *Ar cheart dúinn imeacht?*'

'Agus d'fhreagair an fear eile, *Deoch amháin, go bhfeicfidh muid. Seans go síleann siad gur Sasanaigh muid!* a d'aithris Ganni, ag bualadh an tábla lena lámh le teann gáire.

Lean Manwel leis an scéal.

'Sheas an bheirt acu ansin, ag ól a gcuid dí – iad an-chúramach, ar a bhfaichill. Ní raibh siad cinnte ar chor ar bith ar cheart fanacht nó imeacht. Thuig siad go rímhaith nach raibh muid sásta saighdiúirí a bheith sa bheár. Sa deireadh chuaigh mé suas chucu. *Tommy?* arsa mise, ag díriú ar a gcuid éadaigh. Lig mé orm nach raibh ach cúpla focal agam. *Tommy?* arsa an duine rua. *Nah! Irish. Ireland. Irland!* ar sé, ag díriú a mhéire air féin agus ar an fhear eile. Bhí siad thar a bheith imníoch nach mbeadh muid ag déanamh gur Sasanaigh iad.'

Réaltán Ní Leannáin, *Cití na gCártaí* (Cois Life, 2019).
ISBN: 978-1-907494-93-2
© Réaltán Ní Leannáin & Cois Life
Foilsithe le caoinchead Cois Life

Blobby

Kieran Mc Gurk

Gerhart Anderson Christianson was pretty much it. Rotary Club champion, Golf Club President and Chairman *extraordinaire* of Jaguar Owners Ireland.

'It's the motors they mean,' he boomed. 'I simply couldn't *bear* to keep a big cat in captivity.'

After delegating the tasks in the village hall, on the morning of the village fete there was one spot left and one man left to fill it. Blow-in Gerhart had blundered. He was stuck with dressing up as Mr Blobby.

'It'll help your profile darling. It's a tradition,' whispered his wife. 'Down and dirty with the natives.'

Well, he thought, it would throw up some great pictures on Facebook, could break the ice at the next big party.

The Blobby suit had a fan inside for ventilation and the headpiece distorted the wearer's voice to *Dalek-speak*. It was funny at the start. Gerhart decided to entertain the small children, win them around and therefore the mummies. He *"blobbied"* away to them every way he could think of and carried on and danced his way across the green as far as the bouncy castle, another first for Gerhart.

That was when the youngsters turned into hard little torpedoes and screaming kamikazes. They honed in on his soft spots. One blow from the rear banged his mouth into the cooling fan and sent the batteries tumbling out. A tag team caught him by the neck and he felt the zip scoring a mark on his collar bone. He rolled off the bouncer and lay on the grass for a breather. Gerhart was certain he had a loose crown.

'Oh, Blobby. You're a legend,' gasped a young woman as she threw herself down on the grass beside him and took a selfie. 'The kids'll never forget you."

'I think I'll remember one or two of them myself,' he bleated and slipped away, cross-legged. He tried to remove Blobby's head but the zip wouldn't budge.

'There he is!' shouted the referee of the rugby game. 'You're supposed to put the ball in for the first scrum of the game. It's the tradition.'

Blobby cantered on to the pitch. He could do that much he knew, then seek sanctuary in a quiet dressing room, present the trophy afterwards. But he leant too far into the mass and was swallowed, crammed inside a straining thicket of bone, ligament and studs. He felt as if he was being pulled apart for eating. The scrum carried him twenty yards, slowly, camouflaged by mud and shoulders and shat him out close to the touchline. The junior team was gathered there, sixteen to eighteen-year-old boys still giddy from their victory in the curtain raiser. They knew what Blobby needed.

The man of the match was always dunked in the village stream, but these boys couldn't wait for that nomination. They hoisted Blobby high and trampled towards the humpback bridge.

'Can't swim…please…fraid of water!' was drowned out by a raucous braying of 'Alive alive ohh. ALIVE ALIVE OOOHHOOH,' from the many-throated, multi-peeded beast of celebration at any cost, and *plunge* – Blobby went under, right under to the bottom. He became an ungainly platypus, wriggling and twisting through silt and underwater hair, eventually grabbing rush clumps, sally branches and mouthfuls of air on the side of the river closest to the wood. He would hide out there until the insane fete was over, he decided, and off he went.

He hauled himself on to a dry tree stump. His Blobby headpiece had partially ripped off and lay to one side like an unfinished decapitation. Gerhart wondered if all his hokes and bruises were coalescing into one great sore. He touched a lump on the back of his head before he lay back.

'Bit of ice on that when you go home,' a voice said and the thin, wispy face of the village baker hovered over his. 'They really did give it out this year. You must be *really* unpopular chief.'

'Bloody savages! I seem to have been drawn into some sort of beastly hysteria.'

'Is that what you think? Hmph. I've got a clean robe for you, dry socks and trainers, size nine isn't it chief? Leave Blobby on the tree stump. I always let him dry out there.'

'What do you mean *always*? Has this happened before?'

'It happens every year chief. It's the tradition. In my father's day, it used to be a goat's costume. I think at one time it was a real goat.'

'Are you suggesting I'm some sort of ceremonial scapegoat for the village. How bloody preposterous!'

'I'm saying watch your step chief. You may have the big house, the company too but didn't you blame a junior accountant for a mistake which was yours…last year…got her sacked…poor girl became suicidal almost…til she moved back here… to the village.'

'Listen. It's my company. I'll sack who I want.'

'It's our village. We'll punish who *we* want.'

And so Gerhart had food for thought as he sneaked home, avoiding hostiles, letting himself in with the key hidden outside. He took a long soak, then telephoned his wife.

'I left the fun early,' he oozed. 'Pretty boring really. Listen this is a bit out of the blue but how would you feel about moving?'

Silence.

'They got to you then,' she said. 'Good.'

'You *knew* about this?' he choked.

'Yes…I never said but my grandparents are from the village. I always knew I would have to take you here. Gerhart… I think it's best if you go back to the city and emm…leave the key.'

And thus left Gerhart, gripping his lime-green X-type and a belly full of ibuprofen.

A More Sustainable Future

Karen Mooney

From seed, carefully selected
Only true heritage varieties
Conditions controlled
Air dried in narrow containers
Soaked before being sown into sterile compost

Or perhaps segregated

Planted out, yet never deeply rooted
Dwelling in cultivated beds, pruned
Trained to grow in certain directions.
No rambling, position carefully staked, protected

Or perhaps isolated

A narrow existence, no cross pollination.
My shallow roots could readily be transplanted at the first hint of
frost. Municipal planting at its best

Or perhaps worst

Now, the 'gardeners' who tended me have left.
Perhaps I outgrew them, broke their pots?
I felt vulnerable at first but I have been free to seed
Free to sink roots that entangle with other varieties
Roots that would have previously been pruned
Restricted from straying across boundaries

Or perhaps contained

My tendrils, no longer tied or trained
Free now to explore new structures to lean on, to learn from,
to co-exist with, to support
My roots, no longer contained, now drink from once forbidden
streams
I embrace, I support; I am supported by those who would not have
been permitted into this patch

Or perhaps weeded out

This new landscape, may not be just as tidy,
regimented even, but it is diverse; more sustainable.
It has grown from municipal planting to wild flower meadow
We live together, support each other; roots crossing boundaries;
entangled, they run deeper

Or perhaps stronger. Yes, stronger

A more organic approach now evolving, environmentally friendly
One that supports growth without damage or restriction
One that respects the various species and all of our respective needs.
In turn, we co-exist welcoming more new species to enrich this plot
Future seed to strengthen heritage with diversity
Seed that will germinate for future generations

Perhaps be a more sustainable future?

Shattered

Elaine Toal

It was early one spring morning. Frost still held on, weaving a light lace over the early blooms of spring. I heard a car pull onto the gravel driveway approaching the house slowly. I looked through a corner of the bedroom window and I am frozen, for a moment or for eternity. I am not sure.

I watched her sitting alone in her car watching my house. I knew she did not have a key and I wondered if she would have the nerve to knock. Part of me hoped that she would turn the car around without ever announcing herself.

She and I had parted company many months ago. It was a great friendship spanning decades that was shattered like glass. Our shared past became a million shards of memory on which to prick yourself and bleed. There was no one catastrophic event. It was a series of little things that tapped away at the links that held us together and eventually we set adrift from one another.

She is at the door now, knocking gently at first, but becoming more insistent the longer she stood in the cool of the frosty morning. My curiosity gets he better of me. Wrapping myself in a dressing gown against the pinch of the morning air, I open the door. Her eyes shining with tears, she rushes past me without a word, enjoying the familiarity of my home.

Immediately I am annoyed. Not at her but at myself for letting her do this again. With a deep breath I follow her in and put the kettle on. I wait for her to speak. I busy myself making tea as she sobs and tries to compose herself. I place a cup of tea on the table, strong and sweetened just how she likes it. I say nothing, hoping the silence would press her to speak and to reveal something of the secret that was locked up inside. She reached for the cup, cradling it in her cold hands, enjoying its warmth for a moment. She drew her feet up onto the chair, her chin resting on her knees, sipping her tea. Then she spoke, 'I knew I could come here. I knew you would be here. It's all over with Mark. You were right. He wasn't the one for me.'

I almost laughed. She was the master of understatement. Mark was her employee, and ten years younger. Of course he wasn't the one for her! But I said nothing. She babbled on about the breakup, sipping at her tea, unaware, or perhaps content with, my lack of response. She had come here for a listening ear. I nodded in all the right places, just as she would expect. Eventually she stopped talking. Our teacups were empty, and the spring sun was starting to melt the frost.

But still I felt cold. I waited for her to ask how I was. But that never came. And I realised then that nothing has changed. That we had fallen back into our old familiar pattern. We were two sides of a coin, one domineering, one defeated.

On this day though, something inside me had shifted. Hardened. I did not offer her the hand of friendship she had expected. The silence hung heavy between us. She was waiting for me to mutter some words of comfort. But I was tired of that. I was tired of analysing her and her choices. I was tired of giving advice that was sure to be ignored.

Today she feels the coldness in me and for the first time perhaps she really saw me. With a self-awareness I had never seen in her before, she stood, placing her cup on the table. She looked at me a moment longer than she would usually, and she understood something. 'I shouldn't have come here' she said. I did not argue. She left.

I heard the slam of her car door and the gravel grinding under her wheels. I sighed. It was a deep breath that I did not even know I was holding. There was clarity in that cool spring morning. It was plain to both of us now. That some things when shattered, cannot ever be put back together.

Dílis

Réaltán Ní Leannáin

'Tá mé ag iarraidh bheith i mo Chaitliceach, a Mham.'

Thóg Wendy na pónairí óna hiníon, Lúlú. Seacht mbliana d'aois. Rístuama.

'Agus cad chuige an bhfuil tú ag iarraidh bheith i do Chaitliceach?'

Bhrúigh sí an canna siar go cúl an chófra agus thug sí spléachadh ar an am ar a fón póca. B'fhearr don bheirt acu deifriú le bheith in am do Girls' Brigade.

'Is Caitliceach í Maggie, agus tá an gúna is gleoite amach is amach is amach aici, chonaic mé inné é.'

'Ach níl aici ach an t-aon lá amháin lena chaitheamh, ar ndóigh?'

Shleamhnaigh Wendy an t-anlann Korma isteach sa chófra taobh leis an channa pónairí.

'Domh an próca biatais, a chroí.'

Chroith Lúlú a cloigeann fionn agus shéid sí ribe fánach óna súil.

'Tá sé gleoite ar fad ar fad, agus ní lá amháin atá i gceist. Caitheann sí ar Shatharn an Chéad Chomaoinigh é, agus arís ar an Domhnach an lá dar gcionn, agus ar scoil an Luan sin chomh maith, faoi choinne grianghrafanna, agus, agus...'

'Agus sin é.'

'Is cuma! Tá mé ag iarraidh bheith i mo Chaitliceach! Tá mé ag iarraidh gúna bán! Deir Liam –'

' Ná creid gach focal amach as béal Liam!'

Dingeadh mála rís Basmati idir an t-anlann Korma agus bosca paiprice.

'An bhfeicfimid arís é, a Mham?'

'Aon phrócaí eile fágtha ansin, a chroí?'

'Níl, a Mham. An ndearna muid rúd ínteacht cearr ar Liam?'

D'amharc Wendy idir an dá shúil liatha uirthi.

'Ní dhearna, a thaisce, ní dhearna muidinne rud ar bith cearr ar chor ar bith. Rud ar bith. An cuimhin leat gur imigh Daidí a chónaí le June agus babaí Lindsey?'

'Is cuimhin...'

'Ní dhearna muidinne aon rud ar Dhaidí le go n-imeodh sé, nach ndearna?'

Chroith Lúlú a cloigeann fionn.

'Bhuel, is amhlaidh nach ndearna muid aon rud ar Liam. 'Nois, domh an spaghetti ón mhála sin thall, a stór.'

'Níl cead ag Maggie spaghetti a ithe nuair atá an gúna á chaitheamh aici. An bhfuil spaghetti Protastúnach?'

'Níl, a rún, ní bhíonn bia Caitliceach ná Protastúnach. Níl ann ach go bhfuil Mamaí Mhaggie ag iarraidh an gúna a choinneáil glan nuair nach bhfuil sé ar Mhaggie ach cúpla lá!'

Lig Lúlú osna dhomhain.

'Dá mba agamsa a leithéid de ghúna chaithfinn é gach uile lá dá raibh mé beo'

Tharraing sí anall mála mór prátaí chuig Wendy, agus chuir sí siúd sa chófra faoin doirteal é. Chrom Lúlú isteach chuig cluas a máthara agus rinne sí cogar ann, 'tá péarlaí ar na muinchillí aici!'

'Caithfidh go bhfuil sí iomlán álainn.'

Chrúc Wendy méar tríd an eangach oinniún lena chur sa chuisneoir. Ón taobh eile de dhoras an chuisneora chuala sí an guth beag ag leanstan leis:

'...agus parasol. Sin scáth fearthainne, ach don ghrian. Tá sé bán, fosta, agus rufa agus sequins airgid air. Agus lámhainní. Agus bróga bána. Agus stocaí bána. Agus caille'

Ag brú na bpiobairí isteach i lámh a máthara, thairg sí di cromadh síos. Rinne Wendy amhlaidh agus stán a súile liatha féin isteach i súile liatha caointeacha. 'An dtig liom caille a bheith agam, á Mham, le do thoil? Le do thoil, thoil, thoil?'

Dhruid Wendy na súile ar feadh soicind. Rinne sí macnamh.

'Seo... seo an rud a dhéanfas muid, tá seanchúirtíní net againn sa gharáiste. Déanaimis caille as ceann acu sin, do bharúil?'

Lig Lúlú goldar lúcháire aisti.

'Anois?'

'Chan anois, inniu Déardaoin, lá Girls' Brigade. Nuair a gheobhas muid ar ais abhaile. ... Thig na cúirtíní net a chuartú nuair a bheas GB thart anocht.'

Thiomáin siad ar ais ón chor is ón chasadh ag GB, an carr ar a bhealach abhaile síos, suas droimníní rollacha Ráth Fraoileann. Léim Lúlú amach as an charr le doras an gharáiste a oscailt dá máthair, agus rith sí isteach. Thosaigh sí a thochailt na gcúirtíní net amach as málaí plaistice dubha ar sheilf ar an bhalla cúil.

' ... amharc air seo!' a scréach Lúlú, coróin phlaisteach ina glaic aici a d'oirfeadh do bhanphrionsa.

'Tae ar dtús, tiara ina dhiaidh.'

Bhí muc ar gach mala ag Lúlú, ach ar feadh soicind, díreach. Bhí an choróin i bhfad Uladh ró-loinnireach le smut a choinneáil ar a haghaidh ar feadh i bhfad. Coróin suite ar a cuid coirníní, thug sí faoi mháirseáil mhaorga mhall amach as an gharáiste agus isteach sa chistin.

Excerpt from /Sliocht as *Dílis* le Réaltán Ní Leannáin, Cló Iar-Chonnacht (2015)

Beheaded

Byddi Lee

I recognize your face right away. A year ago your beard might have thrown me off but not now. It's impossible to shave when you can barely move. The neck brace gets in the way, but I dare not remove it. I ignore the itching. Scratching is a gamble – one wrong move, never move again.

Silence enfolds us, drifting with the dust motes, as we face each other in this temporary exhibition in the Armagh County Museum. Damp sounds of traffic slosh in from outside. A muffled cough. A parent hisses urgent whispers to the quick footfalls of a child running where it shouldn't. We hold our tranquillity, united by it, comfortable with it.

I stare. Hardly believing what I see but unable to deny it, your face, there behind the glass, echoes my face.

Do you know me?

Of course, you don't. But I know you.

How am I familiar with your face when my wife is a stranger to me, my kids are aliens, and my parents could be any of the people I see on the street?

Yet, I know you.

The accident snuffed out my memory, a candle-flame between damp finger and thumb. My head is as empty as your skull, you poor sod. My past is a blank screen, all channels off-air, except the one showing the flickering image of broken ice in a muddy pothole and a narrow bicycle wheel spinning to the burr of car horns.

I know you, despite the years, the centuries, the millennia that separate us, regardless of the impossibility of you turning up here, and me seeing you here. I see your face every day, but usually, it looks at me from the bathroom mirror. It's the only place I take time to study it, puzzled, inquisitive and much more animated than right now

28

– but it's the same face always searching mine – always asking the same questions. Who are you? What happened to you? And, now I've found you, I ask you the same questions. Who are you? What happened to you?

I see your injuries, the same as mine, almost.

I read the museum blurb about you. Someone smashed your head, cut it off and threw it in a ditch where it sat for a thousand years. Now, your skull is finally found, but no one understands you – except me, because you could be me.

Did the fracture on your skull whip away your memory too?

No, it ended your life. No induced coma for you. No medication to reduce the swelling of your brain. Your injury was not an accident but a deliberate swing of a weapon, a sword. No brace for your neck.

Where did our memories go?

The woman who says she's my wife interrupts us.

'What's up?' she says, flashing that smile – her way of non-verbally telling me, 'I'm your wife even if you don't remember me.'

But that smile inexplicably raises my hackles.

I'm ashamed of my gut reaction, my anger at her. But if she knows me like she says she does, she'd stop pushing me to remember when I clearly cannot.

Yet, she deserves an effort on my part.

'Look at the facial reconstruction of the skull,' I say, and I point to you.

She hooks her wrist around my elbow and leans in. Her hair falls forward as she peers at you. All I see is the tip of her nose and chin. She unhooks her hand from my elbow and slides long-nailed fingers through her hair, tucking it behind her ear as she cocks her head, looking from you to me.

Maybe it's the bow of her lips stretching straight or the dimple puckering her cheek, or simply the wonderment as she says, 'Oh my goodness! He looks just like you!'

A memory slams into my head, the screen blasts on in vivid Technicolor.

She's looking at our baby boy, just born and saying the same words.

And I remember! I remember that first staggering sense of love, protectiveness and tenderness for our child, hers and mine.

29

More pictures, thoughts, memories unfurl and carpet my mind.

The first moment I met my wife and life blossomed with longing and love.

The coffin my father was laid to rest in, and the drag of his loss.

My sister making me laugh like no one else can, making my beautiful kids laugh the same way.

My mother's perfume – the scent of comfort, home.

Like old friends, my memories repopulate and the files on the people I love replenish.

You smile.

I turn, do a double-take before realising that it's my reflection on the glass overlaid on your face that's smiling.

'Maybe he's your ancestor,' she says.

'Perhaps.'

I hook my little finger around hers – our special way of holding hands.

Her eyes widen.

She knows.

I know.

Zaragoza

Kieran Mc Gurk

I was drowsy, but looking back, I did notice how people moved away
from her. The lacy figure glided along the platform then stopped at
the display cases behind me; crystal, porcelain and those ornamental
daggers Zaragoza was famous for. She liked things behind glass. She
definitely liked me. As she sat down, the cockerel cries of a porter
faded as if some sort of soft door had been closed. I hadn't spoken
to a soul in days and couldn't remember when I last slept. My *band*
had been touring the Basque country and the night before last was
when I walked. A shitty bar with no stage and an owner who
wouldn't let us play when he saw we were metal. He said our gear
would use too much electricity. He'd booked a folk band he said.
That's what the promoter told him he said.

 She had the tiniest scent bottle in the palm of her hand and whisper-
sang to the air of *Freres Jacques*,

    'Zaragoza, Zaragoza
Choo choo choo
Do do do
Forget about the train child
Forget about the train child
I'm with you
I'm with you.'

    My head sank to her lap. I looked up into her face, her green
eyes and the tiny scar over her left eyebrow like an upside-down
question mark.

    When I woke up I was surrounded by armed militia, cable-tied
and hoofed off to a holding cell. I genuinely thought the blood on
my hands and my jacket was from a nosebleed. I suffer those from
time to time. The coke, I think.

'I didn't know Jose Dominguez,' I pleaded. 'I've never been to his hotel! Can I have a lawyer? Someone who speaks proper English?'

'Ah, Senor. Ze blood. Ze dagger. Yor preents. Dominguez has zee nice girls. Yo not pay heh? He get angry, heh?'

The detective held a nine by seven, black and white picture up to the bars. Just one. It showed the back of a man's head, grey, balding, skewered through the ears to a desk by a thin, silver dagger with a diamanté hilt. A printer coughed in an office close by. He set the picture on the floor for me then walked away. The image was compelling, more familiar than I would admit, and I was glad I couldn't see the victim's face.

The detective returned with a swagger. He had an A4 sheet in his hand.

'You musician heh? Heavy metal heh? Eeempaler. What ees Eeempaler?'

He pointed at the logo on the reverse of my biker jacket.

'*Im* paler. It's my band. It's just a shortened version of Vlad the Impaler...you know… Dracula n' all.'

'And thees?'

He turned around the sheet. It was a copy of the back cover of our one and only album, *Nothing but Blood*; a skull impaled through the ears by a dagger with a jewelled handle. He set it on the floor beside the photograph and walked away.

The next time I saw the detective was in the courtroom. A special arraignment was called for just after midnight, to get in front of a hungry press pack. The judge didn't like publicity, had a certain way of doing things. I was told this by a creased-up sort of a man, tiny but well fed, with a tongue which leeched out hints of brandy every time he spoke. He was infuriatingly slow with his translation and found my predicament disturbingly entertaining. This was my solicitor.

We all waited in Court No 2. The room was much smaller than I had expected. I made several attempts to relate my story to my brief but he waved me down. Worse than that he laughed and laughed until I stood up to make a plea for more capable representation. Everyone else stood up too and for a moment I felt they were on my side. Then the policeman I was cuffed to hissed at me to be silent. A panel on the front wall opened and a staccato voice from the bench announced the arrival of the most honourable Judge Estemondo.

She glided onto her throne and when she sat down we all followed suit. I looked across at her green eyes and the scar above her left eyebrow like an upside-down question mark.

Three weeks later my insanity plea was accepted. Judge Estemondo is patron of the Zaragoza Manicomio. That's an asylum to you and me. That's where she keeps her collection. She likes things behind glass.

A Smile

Eddie McClenaghan

Una's smile usually beamed from ear to ear. Even when she lost her baby teeth and her family teased her about boys kissing all her teeth out, her gummy smile was adorable.

That's what her mummy had thought anyway.

Not anymore.

Una, 14 now, didn't smile much around her family anymore. Instead, she gritted her teeth when she wasn't allowed to go out that weekend or whenever her Dad bugged her to get up for school.

'Do you know what time it is Una?'

'Urrrghh…DoI look like a clock?'

'Come on. The bus'll be away!'

Today was picture day. Una had been a selfie addict since she was 13, but not today. Not when you've had your pearly whites clamped with train track braces.

'Naw ye look more like a cheese grater.' Her twin brother Ronan never missed a trick.

'Shut *up*! Daddy, I've had to listen to crap like this from everyone at school all week! Why'd I have to get these stupid braces?'

Una heard the names. 'Braceface'. How original. Then there was the collective chattering of teeth complimented by the WOO-WOOOO train sounds. On the bus. In her class. At break-times. All day. Every day. She couldn't even escape it at home. They sent Snapchats doing the same thing too.

'It's only for another few weeks, pet. Look, come down here and get your breakfast, both of you, before you miss that bus! Unless you want a lif–'

'NOOO'. Una and Ronan cried in unison.

'Not the loser cruiser!' Una couldn't be seen rolling up to the school gates in her Dad's Renault Modus again. The obnoxious green septic tank on wheels had already made one appearance at school and it was one too many.

'Well, it's that or the bus, up to you.'

'I'm not going!' Una shouted down the stairs. She heard the growing thump of her dad's work-boots trekking up the stairs.

Una heard Dad drawing breath, as he towered above her.

She felt his hand on her shoulder. Una shifted herself around the other way to look up at him for a second before looking at the ceiling and squinting back her tears.

'Pet, it's okay. It's just one photo. You have a beautiful smile, your mother's smile, thank God. When I smile, I look like I'm having a stroke!'

Not even a smirk from Una.

'You don't have to show your teeth to smile, ye know. A good smile is in the eyes anyway. And look at yours, beautiful blue eyes. You have your mother's eyes too, thanks be to God. If you had mine...'

'It's not even the picture, Daddy...I can put up with that crap. It's...' Una couldn't finish her sentence before tears again. She looked back at her Dad's welled up eyes. He must've seen the family photo she had open on her phone – Una, Ronan, Dad and Mum on holidays in the Lake District. Five years ago to the day. Una remembered that day. The beautiful holiday cottage they stayed in with the sweet old landlady who gave them sweets and ice cream. The scenic views on their family walks together. Swimming and racing against Ronan to crown the fastest twin.

He always said he was first to be born but her Mum told her it was really her by three minutes and that she just said that to Ronan to keep him quiet. She'd never forget how Mum smiled at her then. How she smiled for that photo. She was such a glamorous lady. Una couldn't help but smile herself when people said she looked like her Mum.

Una would never forget her mother's smile.

But she'd never forget her Mum's screams either, and whatever the hell that thing was.

Una still didn't know. None of her family did. All they could do was watch as her Mum was pulled into the water. She'd never forget those teeth. Razor sharp, twisted teeth. Like something that could do

35

with braces more than her. She'd never forget how it looked straight at her from those hollow dark eyes; smiling.

Her Dad sat with her and hugged her tight. Una heard the bus driving down the road past her bedroom window. She felt another arm around her shoulder. A twin sized arm.

Even with her family's arms around her, she missed the warmth of the pair that weren't there anymore. She'd never forget her Mum's hug.

Armagh

Mark Brownlee

A place where saints and scholars made their home,
yet you and I now live in homes apart
where spires great adorn horizon's line,
but you and I now meddle in our feuds.

Where streets bend through the solid brick
and we flow freely through them now as one
like blood inside a single body's vein
yet we bleed green or orange never red.

Here Patrick built his church upon a hill
for Christians there to make it cardinal.
This cross-shaped edifice of ochre stone
the place of my religion but not yours.

Your gothic church is on another hill
a larger structure, with two steeples great
each like an angel guarding you within,
but carefully they watch me there without.

We look for a leader who'll unite
a noble king of old lies here to rest
uniting our whole island for a time
he then was buried in my church, not yours.

For we make our claims over diff'rent men
like he who fought for this great ancient land
at the place of Navan Fort and mound
where this hound of Ulster once did reside.

There your forefathers ancient, great and wise
spoke myths and lore from out their memories depths
'Cuchulain' is the loud shout that they cry
But we fight to make our claim over him.

We turn to reason and to libraries
mine is a great Georgian library house
While yours a modern house of lit'rature
for we are sep'rate in our learning here.

We both love football but have diff'rent rules
Soccer, Gaelic call it what you will.
Divergently we go to sights of sport,
which stand in our sep'rate communities.

But we share the same moon, stars, sun and sky
and our Planetarium is for all
where we both marvel at the glory seen
which lifts us up above our petty feuds.

When darkened heaven radiates its light
a hundred million eyes watch and discern
at reasons why we argue and dispute
But the celestial bodies are aloof.

The centre of our city is the Mall
where crimson orb is thrown to lowered bat
where people walk in and out of its place
like tiny cells inside a human heart.

There are memorials, to those who died
for British kings, you never called your own
but for a city that we cherish now
and that is the thing that will unite us both.

Hunter's Moon O'er Airgialla

Rosemary Tumilty nee Lavery

Synopsis of Hunter's Moon O'er Airgialla

The stage play, *Hunter's Moon O'er Airgialla*, opens in present day Ireland and focuses on the turmoil faced by the majority of people of these ancient lands where now lays a border, and the uncertainty that surrounds their lives as they stand poised on the cusp of Brexit.

The lead character, Rebecca, a feisty English-speaking Goth troubadour inadvertently invokes the wit, will and wisdom of the 18th century Irish poets, scholars and Bards of Creggan in South Armagh, and, in a brief interlude, we are transported back in time to 1744 to witness the reality of Ascendancy Rule and the Penal Laws set against the backdrop of the Jacobite rebellion. We rely on Rebecca, who has taken on the mantle of Macha, the ancient Celtic warrior goddess, to bring understanding, knowledge and sapience to bear on our present position in the 21st century.

The play is to be launched in 2019 as a tribute to these great Irish Bards, Art Mac Cumhaigh, Peadar O'Doirnin, Padraig Mac A Liondain and Seamus Mor Mac Mhurchaidh, and is set to commemorate the 250th anniversary of the passing of Peadar O'Doirnin (1769), and in 2020 the 300th anniversary of the birth of Seamus Mor Mac Mhurchaidh, and in 2023 the 250th anniversary of the passing of Art Mac Cumhaigh, as well as the 290th anniversary for Padraig Mac A Liondain.

Hunter's Moon O'er Airgialla

A Play in One Act by Rosemary Tumilty nee Lavery

(Ghosts of 18th century poets in italics: Art Mac Cumhaigh, Peadar O'Doirnin, Padraig Mac A linden and Seamus Mac Mhurchaidh)

Setting - Present day: Creggan Graveyard, dusk on a chilly All Hallows' Eve.

Rebecca stands in Creggan graveyard, hand poised on Art Mac Cumhaigh's icy gravestone, pondering to herself on life, past and present. Initially she is oblivious to any voices from beyond the grave, until she falls, and catastrophe strikes.

A short excerpt from Act I: Scene 1.

So! All Hallows Evening. Huh! My very own Bloomsday 2019,
Near the Vault of The O'Neill's Clan, on Creggan's hallowed ground.
Curiosity my compass, inquisitiveness my yoke,
Foot jolts near frozen headstones: my neck - so dear - near broke!

The Rectory walled garden, guess I'd better see it soon, as
I've examined all the headstone slabs, but not yet seen the O'Neill's tomb.
Darkness then descending, along with frost and freezing fog,
Returning from the Poets Trail, crossing river, streams and bog.

Each gravestone paying homage - to a life long gone,
The Eighteenth Century, still somehow hanging on;
A labyrinth of history as lives unfold,
In death these men lie side by side; in life, adversaries exposed.

Irish Celts and Bards galore! Talk of moral codes, and Brehon Law!
Seventeen and forty-four (1744) – The Jacobite Rebellion, and The
French at our door.
Fragile truce amongst Airgialla Clans, up and around Slievegullion
lands,
But war, as ever, to erupt. People – so impoverished! The Courts – so
corrupt!

- Ah - My hand rests upon Mac Cumhaigh's grave, a humble Celtic
cross
Embossed with words transcending time: a message from The Gods.
Then opening gates to O'Neill's vault, perhaps a tiny peek?
For 70 skulls, a Clan so felled: truth and wisdom do I seek!

The slow drawn-out sigh, and wavering cry:
Gated hinge-joints as old - as the very dawning of time!

Fírinne agus eagna – Ha! - Is that 'all' you seek?
Céard faoi grá, agus onóir?
Go speak of foresight with Byzantine Greeks;
For the notion of prudence: it doth wander!

An eerie silence prevails.
Irish lives stolen, Irish lives spent: from the past, we search the truth
To understand that which has gone before, no fountain of eternal
youth!
The here and now determined, a future to shape, to form, to mould;
These Bards have impact upon my life, my time: Teachings, as yet
untold.

To question us, in your hour of need! Be gone and bother us not!
You're meddling with that which you do not understand;
As for us - we're done with life's melting pot!

Silence still, no-one about! I might as well keep on going.

So, in the Vault descending, one step, then another,
Entering the depths of time, depths of Earth: our Mother.
Sludge 'pon steps beneath my feet: Suddenly I'm tumbling! Tossing!
Turning!
Bone strikes stone, and to musty earth I fall!
Blood from my temple weeping! Burning!

Indeed, to question Us, in your hour of need!
Which of us is it, that you shall heed?
For war will beckon the hearts of men,
Whilst you dabble and plunge with your world-weary pen!

Or should people's hearts fly, on Love's fickle wing;
Or feet rooted in ground, from where saplings shall spring?
Audacity now, to question us still! Does this woman know no limits!
Fine! Fine! Let's gather our robes!
To find answers, they send us Her, of all women!

So, to another world I wake, of fog, and freezing mist;
Shadowed figures gliding by: to the river, they will not desist.
They each hold out a ghostly hand, draped in cloth of muslin;
A Hunter's Moon shines from above. Why I take their hands I cannot
fathom.

Walk with us. Walk with us, 'neath the gleam of the Hunter's Moon!
Gealach sealgaire! Oh! Gealach sealgaire! La Luna Del Cacciatore!

Hunter's Moon! Oh! Hunter's Moon! Oh - Dio Mio! Mi Amore!

So, it is down by the river, the gathering,
'Neath a silver gilded moon reflected on the water;
Creggan River through stone had hewn.
Ne'er earth, nor sod, nor tombstone slab,
could hush a poet's message,

For spectral voice, when you least expect;
will dance in chorus, and in passage.

The whisper of their footfall, 'pon leaves of hallowed ground,
For confines of a burial stone, could not presume to keep them
down!
Shimmering Bards rooted, reflections 'pon the water:
One big, one small, one barely there, and one reflected not at all!

For I fear that I am dreaming, and not really here at all,
I search, for, in their wisdom, I know in my heart 'twas me they did
call!

Come down from oft that leafy path; join us, for the time is soon!
Such lamb's eyes! You'll be bleating, 'neath the gleam of the Hunter's Moon!

Sassenach og! Croi og! Intinn og!
Do you truly see, the pillage and the murder, plundering of our seed?
Can't get us out! They'll breed us out! Bloodlines weakened, torn asunder!
From O'Neill's Vault 70 skulls - Rise Up! They ne'er made it o'er to
Connaught.

'Righteous Queen! Helen of Troy!' Mac Cumhaigh weeping; falls to his
knees!
Despair grips the proceedings, facing Seamus Mor do I simply freeze!
For his hefty, foreboding presence, stills the air: I bow, I shake!
His words do chill and haunt me; standing eye to eye, in this
glistening nook:

We'll Raise 'you' up high, we'll Set 'you' down under;
Carry 'you' to Carnally & lay 'you' in the barn below!
For that river is as our troubled lives:
O'er ridge, and stone, and boulder.

43

Could she be my 'Flower of Maidens, Le hUr Chnoc Chein Mhic Cainte?
Do you think she'll carry our message? I'll search her eyes, her soul, her face!

Peadar's hand reaches from the depths of time, brushes my cheek,
lifts a tear;
But a calmness has come over me: there is nothing here to fear.
Exchange of words, and thoughts, and minds, within this mystic
place;
'Cross realms of time, and space, and mass: clear user interface.

Gealach sealgaire! Oh! Gealach sealgaire! La Luna Del Cacciatore!
Hunter's Moon....Hunter's Moon. Dio Mio, Mi Amore.

The bells ring out! For whom they toll? For you? Or I? Or they?
But in the mists of mind and time Bards dissipate and fade away.

Come back! Where are you going?
Quo Vadis Anam Cara? Do not leave,
For we have much to ponder;
On life, on love, on all mankind,
For time we shall not squander.

Quo Vadis friend? Do not heed the call!
For gravity doth beckon,
To pull you down to its own heart:
Grave beats will surely deafen;

Lethargy it's weapon!
Quo Vadis Anam Cara?
Quo Vadis?

One More

Malachi Kelly

The last of the lights went out plunging the street into an untimely death. His eyes scraped at the darkness. Sinister shadows made from innocent objects stretched across his path and newspaper headlines appeared like flashes in front of him.

As his eyes became accustomed to the blackness his step became stronger, quicker, of more purpose.

He had stayed too long at his girlfriend's house. The effort to leave was compounded by the encroaching winter weather and the warmth of her arms.

Digging his hands deep into his duffle coat pockets and thinking of which route home he should take he disappeared into the maze of side streets and small estates, eerily quiet bar the odd barking dog.

The igniting of the car engine broke the silence which the three had held for the last ten minutes signalling the start of their nights 'work'.

For one of them it was his first 'job' but at seventeen he wasn't the youngest in his position. The engine purred, its full petrol tank indicated on the luminous dashboard.

Their route had been chosen earlier in the day to avoid the collection of roadworks which were in progress around the city.

Neatly indicating, and with the headlights on dip, the car slowly moved out of the side street to join the few remaining vehicles still on the roads.

His thoughts were on his girlfriend and how she seemed to hold him closer than usual before he left. He felt good inside thinking about her and about their future.

He was in love.

The determined step he fell into had warmed his feet and as he came out onto the central thoroughfare he started whistling.

Street lights worked in this part of the city and as he approached what during the day was a busy junction his eyes instinctively scanned the adjoining dark side streets. He turned left and walked away from the junction, continuing on the main road.

It was at this point that he noticed the car coming towards him in the far side lane. His mind ran through what was now a habitual procedure at this time of night: Make of car, colour, registration, speed, number of occupants, windows up or down.

Ford Cortina, Dark blue or black, HLZ 39..., normal speed, two – no – three occupants, windows up.

He watched out of the corner of his eye as the car passed and drove on. He breathed more easily, his safety procedure over for now.

The click of the 'safety' on the 9mm automatic pistol was deafening to the seventeen-year-old. Beads of sweat appeared like raindrops over his brow and bridge of his nose. The mask when he pulled it over his head, swept the perspiration into his eyes.

They slowed at the junction indicating to come back down the same street, all the time aware of drawing attention to themselves.

By now the windows of the Cortina were misted from the heat of the bodies, the 17yr's old especially.

He was in the back passenger seat, his hand pulling frantically at the window winder. 'It won't open! The fuckin' window won't open!' The driver instantly reduced speed but didn't drop gear for fear of alerting their target, which was now barely one hundred and fifty yards away.

Under frantic efforts of both passengers, the stiff window began to give and fully opened within a hundred yards.

But this irritation in their plan had the effect of wrecking the youth's nerve. His hands shook violently.

Whatever it was – instinct, experience, survival – his sense of danger became very real as the sound of the car slowed.

He turned and looked back up the road.

Dark blue Cortina, back nearside window open and what seemed like an arm or a hand protruding slightly.

He had stopped now, as had time.

Once again newspaper headlines flashed through his mind. A sick, choking feeling came to his throat as he made out the shape of a gun at the window. Frozen, he was unable to do a damned thing as the car was merely yards away.

The armed youth was crying. Not from sorrow, but fright, anger, frustration and a loathing of himself. He raised his hand and tried to steady his aim but could not control himself. By now he was shaking all over and in that same instant, his eyes met his target's. It seemed like an eternity as his mind took in every detail in that petrified, disbelieving face; the face of an innocent, terrified seventeen-year-old.

Far in the distance a voice, a whisper at first, but then an order, a command, roaring, 'Shoot you bastard! Shoot the bastard!'

Automatically he aimed at those eyes, which were all that he could see, and closing his own, he fired twice.

L'Origine du Monde Speaks

P.V. Wolseley

Gustave said, 'I want to tell the truth,' but I suspected a cover-up: he kept saying to the model, 'No one will know it's you.' When he said, '*C'est fini!*' I wanted to say, '*Ce n'est pas fini!* My torso's twisted!' but of course I couldn't – Gustave had made sure of that. Whatever truths he wanted to tell, they weren't the model's, or mine.

At first I was exposed only for occasional private viewings. I remember fabric being drawn back. A look. A touch. Whispered desires – not mine, obviously.

Now I'm on public display, people mutter instead about my title, brushstrokes and pigments, but few take the time to really examine them. Even if they do, their gaze always returns to the same spot. And no one mentions my back.

Some visitors pretend they've stumbled across me by accident. Others sidle up as if I might bite. If my lips could speak, I'd ask, 'What are you so scared of?'

Occasionally feminists march up and talk loudly about liberation. At first I thought, 'This lot will do something for my back,' but it soon became clear that they had their own agenda; some talked without even looking at me.

Sometimes, a sensitive soul stands before me and asks, 'Who was she? How did she feel? What she was thinking?' But even as I lie legs akimbo, I can only keep my secrets; the part of me that could tell is forever falling out of the frame.

L'Origine du Monde Speaks was first published by *Flash Frontier* in 2014

A Thick Foundation

Byddi Lee

Strawberry jam spread right to the corners on fluffy white squares, exactly how George liked them.

A picky eater, even as a baby, he'd screw up his little red face as he mouthed around for her nipple and pummeled her with tiny pink fists. His furtive squawks made her hands shake. When he'd finally latched on, he'd gulp down all she had to offer and she'd watch him with pride and relief.

Her wee son – the light of her life.

Her hand juddered when she lifted his plate so it clacked against the Formica countertop. She switched it to her good hand and set it on the kitchen table in front of George.

'Here you go, love. Will we switch off the telly?'

'The football's on.' George looked at the plate. 'What's that?'

'Just a wee bite to keep you going.'

'I'm not eating that.' He shoved the plate to the middle of the table.

'But you're a growing boy.'

'Ma, I'm thirty- seven.'

Kathleen sniffed, reached across, picked up the plate and carried it to the counter. There was no space to set it down. The breakfast dishes piled by the sink. She would wash up once the shaking settled down. Her hand was playing up because she was letting tiredness and stress get to her.

 She set the bread and jam, plate and all, into the cupboard, somewhere he couldn't see it, somewhere it wouldn't upset him.

'Maybe you'll stay for dinner?'

She had a steak in the fridge. A treat for herself, but if George wanted it…

'Nah, I'm going out.'

'With Megan?'

'No. We're finished. Sure I told you that. Jesus, ma, you never listen!'

'Right, right. Sorry. I remember now.' But she didn't.

She rested her hand on his shoulder. His flesh pushed at his shirt, fat and squidgy beneath her fingers. She thought of his father, the same age, white-faced, clutching his chest.

'I saw her up the town on Wednesday,' Kathleen said. She held her breath.

George straightened up, twisting in his chair to look her in the eye. 'So?'

'Well, she was plastered in make-up.' His interest in what she was saying gave her courage to go on. 'It did her no favours neither. Her foundation looked like she laid it on with a gardening trowel.'

'Plaster's trowel, ma.'

'Right well, anyway, she'd these ludicrous big sunglasses on her like you see them film-star ones wearing. Made her look like a bug.'

George turned his gaze to the floor.

'You'll meet a nicer girl, son.' The poor soul was devastated. Her heart sank. When George hurt, she hurt.

'I do not want to discuss it,' George said through clenched teeth.

Kathleen took the steak from the fridge and brought it to the hob. She used her good hand to turn on the ring, but the shakes picked up in the bad hand so the pan rattled against the cooktop.

'What are you doing?'

'I'm making you a nice steak,' she said.

'I told you, I don't want anything!'

'But a nice wee bit of—' She turned toward him. The pan flipped sideways, the steak slid out and landed on the lino with a glop.

'Jesus, ma, look what you've done now.'

'Sorry, son. I just—'

'Stop shaking that pan around,' George towered over her, his eyes bulging.

Kathleen let go of the pan. It clattered into the sink, knocking down a pile of dishes and smashing a glass.

'See, this is what happens when you don't clean up after yourself. Ya stupid bitch!' Spittle flew from his lips, wetting her cheeks.

She lifted her hands to her face, the bad one flip-flopping like a fish on a line. 'I'm sorry…'

George bared his teeth, and darkness swallowed the last of the light in his eyes. His red face screwed up, as he mouthed obscenities. Not-so-tiny fists pummeled the flesh that had once nourished them.

It's not his fault. He's stressed out. He just broke up with his girlfriend. His father died young. He doesn't mean it.

Pain forced her mind from her body.

Kathleen came to on the lino beside the steak.

Jerky and shivering, she pushed herself into a sitting position. The black mirror of the oven door bounced her reflection back to her. Her trembling fingers explored the ballooning eyebrow.

Kathleen stared at the dark image of herself. She'd have to take time off work, lose out on earnings and hide from her friends for a week or more this time. Unless…and she wondered…where Megan had gotten her thick foundation and those big sunglasses.

Cás na dteifeach – Tá dhá thaobh ar an bhád

Seán Ó Farraigh

Ar chóir dúinn na daoine seo a fhágáil ar an trá fholamh?
Ná hinis dom mar sin de
B'fhéidir go dtiocfadh leis na haghaidheanna cráite seo bheith cosúil linne
Má bhí saol eile i ndán dúinn
Caithfidh muid na cineálacha daoine atá iontu a nochtadh
Na haidiachtaí leisciúla sprionlaithe a chur orthu
Gan aon amhras, níor chóir dúinn
Fáilte a chur rompu
Ba chóir dúinn rogha amháin a thabhairt dóibh
Dul ar ais chun na dtíortha as a tháinig siad
Níl siad in ann
Ár gcuid tithe a roinnt
Ár gcuid bia a roinnt
Ina áit, b'fhearr dúinn
Constaic ollmhór a thógáil chun iad a dhíbirt
Níl sé ceart ná cóir
Cosúlachtaí a dhéanamh eadrainn
Ní áibhéil ar bith go dtig le duine
Amharc ar an saol i ndóigheanna áirithe
Déan é

Léigh ón bhun anois

The Power of a Peeler

Trish Bennett

The Mother-in-law has a potato peeler. 'So what?' you say, but when you hear she never goes anywhere without it, you start to wonder. She upped sticks at sixty five and headed on a whirlwind tour of the world, with only her culinary companion for company.

That peeler has gallivanted more than most. It toured the Himalayas with the sherpas in Nepal ('well you'd never know when you might need to peel something') and travelled Australia and the US. I wouldn't be surprised if it was used as a defensive weapon by the Mother-in-law against the advances of a lusty 17 year old Egyptian who cornered her in the alleyway near his fathers jewellery shop.

In the past few years the new FAA regulations have meant the trusty tool cannot travel to far flung places with its owner anymore. Worried that something might happen to her most valuable possession, my mother in law places it and its twin (a spare one, just in case) under protective custody in a safe.

I used to laugh about it all thinking it was one of those follies that 'ladies of a certain age' pursue. She arrived home after one of her many adventures with a wee present for me. A potato peeler. I think it was bought in Italy or France and carried home with several siblings nestled in the trusty leather handbag, beside the passport and gold jewellery. When I unwrapped the peeler from its packaging I knew I was finally accepted into the inner sanctum of family, no longer quite the outlaw.

At the time I thanked her and put it into the drawer that everyone has, the one containing things you rarely use. One flustered day I couldn't find my regular peeler and resorted to rooting in the drawer. I grabbed the mother-in-laws peeler and horsed into the nearest potato. It was a devil to get used to it, I had to make several adjustments to my normal peeling angle to get into the swing of it. Before I knew it, the dinner vegetables were in the pot and on the boil. A neat pile of slim shavings smiled up at me from the compost bucket. The peeler was moved to a position of power in the kitchen — the utensils jar beside the cooker.

Over time, I realised I had been 'turned'. I finally came to terms with my obsession when I found myself buying and hiding a spare peeler of the same type, in case someone took the original. When I moved house the peeler was not packed into a storage box with the kitchen items, but carried carefully in a secret pocket in the handbag.

I wasn't the only one she converted following that trip. During a family holiday, my husband spotted my sister-in-law and her boyfriend, a normally easy going couple, arguing over whose turn it was to use the 'good' peeler. The argument was heated and all stayed well away until peace was restored when they took turns sharing use of the powerful utensil.

On a recent trip to my own Mothers house, I found myself cursing her potato peeler. I was digging gouges out of the spuds, and taking far too long getting the dinner on. My Mother pushed me aside with a 'tut', took hold of the peeler, and flew through the potatoes quicker than a nun through customs. I muttered defeated about the 'rubbish peeler'. She laughed at me saying that was 'nonsense', I just didn't know how to use it. She then stripped down the peeler with the speed of a sniper after a kill. 'It can be dismantled for travel' she said.

Often, I find myself scouring the kitchen utensils section in shops. I justify my search saying I'm looking for a spare peeler for my mother-in-law (who still mourns the loss of one of hers, despite all her safeguards).

Have I gone mad?

Have I reached that 'certain age' too?

Maybe I'm under just under influence of a truly magical kitchen device.

Previously published: March 2018, Recorded by Lisburn 98 FM for *Lisburn Reads*. November 2016, *The Leitrim Guardian* 2017. Jul 2016, BBC Radio Ulster *Time of Our Lives.* June 2013, *Ireland's Own*.

After the Conflict

Peter Hollywood

After the conflict, huge, mechanical cranes suddenly overarched the city centre skyline and skips appeared in the suburbs.

Property prices soared, after the conflict, and most people stopped moving house. Instead, they renovated; there were loft conversions and kitchen extensions; front gardens were often slabbed over, gravelled or interred in tarmacadam to make secure parking space for one or both cars. There were hagglings and horse-tradings with architects and surveyors, negotiations with planning services; tenders sought from small construction companies, whose small, dirty vans were seen buzzing about everywhere. Loans arranged; re-mortgagings. Lawyers and barristers managed to move house. Elsewhere there were rows over boundary lines and deeds produced from nowhere; cans of white spray X-ing driveways and walls with what looked like badly applied band-aids.

After the conflict, you could hardly get a plumber or plasterer for love or money; some brave souls had a go at it themselves.

In the suburbs there were Kangos and Bobcats, and long lorries, loaded with red brick and breeze blocks, Rosemary tiles or Bangor Blues; setts and cobbles: Cedar, Heather, Charcoal and Bracken; Old Court flags or textured and riven flags, Sandstone circular and kerbsetts: Autumn Brown, Sage Green, Sahara. There was traffic congestion in small avenues and closes, courts and cul de sacs.

Daylight burst down, Bible-like, after the conflict, through apertures in roofs made for the insertion of Vellux skylights and dark and dust scurried off on four legs and eight for cover under the suddenly exposed joists, purlins and rafters. Wasp-nests were detonated, swallows and swifts and bats put to flight.

Avenues clanged with the sound of industry. Little corner shops did a brief boom trade in cigarettes and sandwiches, high energy drinks and newspapers, Mars bars and teabags. Urban foxes poked their noses into suddenly overloaded yellow skips. Dog-walkers strolled past and peered inquisitively into the rash of miniature building sites, taking notes, inspecting, making comparisons and simply satisfying their own curiosity. On dry, windy days, there were mini sand-storms and tarpaulins flapped and slapped loudly; plastic carry-out coffee cups and torn plastic sheets, fangs of white polystyrene got ensnared in people's hedges and neighbours complained about the mess the street was in and the health and safety implications of badly illuminated skips at night. People peered out through double glazing, conservatories. Orangeries.

All the time, downtown, the construction continued apace. Old buildings that had survived the conflict got make-overs and face-lifts or were torn down and demolished; making way for the new. CCTV sniffed the air.

Meanwhile, a smarter class of helicopter began to buzz the skies above us, lighter and brightly bubbled and often with a corporate logo emblazoned on the fuselage. Police cars too became candied and colourful. Helmets and flap-jackets were mostly shed. For a brief season, youths purchased pink and lilac kaki coloured combats from high street stores.

Talk of betrayal began to fade from beer-soaked, heated bar-room debate replaced instead with words such as amnesty and reconciliation; the obfuscating fug of cigarette smoke lifted too with that ban.

So, from Canada and America came ice-hockey players; plasterers and plumbers from Eastern Europe, furniture from Sweden. Then, also from America, sub-prime mortgages became a topic of vexed conversation along with the associated fear of a credit crunch so that property prices took a tumble and people continued to… mostly stop moving house. In floodplains, wise residents moved sockets higher up their walls and demanded more regular purgation of drains. Many retained sodden sand-bags; just in case. There was talk of climate change.

However, out in the countryside, someone was setting age-old Orange Halls alight and hoax devices were being found tethered to railings around rural Gaelic playing fields. It appeared dark men were still meeting in late places.

Yet the people are resilient; it is after the conflict now and they renovate and home-improve, extend, redecorate and all the time appreciate the city and its transformations; but every-so-often, in the midst of this flurry of activity, some might stop and look around them. Watch them. Periodically, they will pause and, for a moment, hesitate as if unsure of this normality. It might be the hawk shadow of a low-cost airplane passing overhead or the hollow boom of an empty skip being clumsily dumped to the ground. It might simply be the lack of noise; silence.

Whatever, they will look around; then, when reassured, they'll proceed about their business.

After the Conflict is from the collection *Hawks and Other Short Stories* published by New Island Books.

Lugh ag Teacht i gCabhair ar Chúchulainn

Réamonn Ó Ciaráin

Ar maidin, chonaic Laogh fear ag teacht ionsorthu tríd an champa ón taobh thoir thuaidh.

'Tá fear ag teacht inár dtreo, a Chú bhig óig, fear ard dathúil agus lonrú air. Tá fallaing ghlas thart air ceangailte le bróiste airgid. Tá léine shíoda le bróidnéireacht d'ór dearg air, a thiteann a fhad lena ghlúine. Tá sciath dhubh le himeall de chré-umha bhán ina lámh agus sleá chúig bheann ina lámh eile. An rud is aistí, áfach, nach dtugann aon duine i gcampa Éireann an fear seo faoi deara.'

'Más amhlaidh,' arsa Cúchulainn, 'mura dtig le fir Éireann é a fheiceáil, tá a fhios agam go maith cé atá ann. Cara liom den lucht sí atá tagtha i gcabhair orm, mar tá a fhios aige go maith nach bhfuil sé furasta seasamh leat féin i gcoinne ceithre chúige.'

Tháinig Lugh Lámhfhada ón slua sí a fhad le Cúchulainn agus labhair leis. Bhí a fhios aige go raibh Can laoch seo scriosta leis an troid agus leis an tuirse.

'Codail leat anois, a Chú chróga,' arsa Lugh, 'agus coinneoidh mé féin faire mhaith ort go ceann trí lá agus trí oíche.'

Tháinig tonn bháite chodlata thar Chúchulainn. Thit sé ina chnap codlata in aice le huaigh Learga. Ní nárbh ionadh mar bhí sé ag troid sula raibh féile na Samhna ann gan chodladh seachas tamall beag anseo is ansiúd ar thaca a shleá. Le linn dó a bheith ina chodladh go trom, chuir Lugh lusanna draíochta ar a chuid chneácha. Chneasaigh siad uilig. Nuair a bhí trí lá agus trí oíche codlata caite ag Cúchulainn, d'éirigh sé agus chuimil a aghaidh. Líonadh le cumhacht agus le misneach arís é. Tháinig fonn bia agus dí air agus shantaigh sé cuideachta agus cairdeas mná.

'Cá fhad a bhí mé i mo chodladh?' a d'fhiafraigh sé.

'Trí lá agus trí oíche,' arsa Lugh.

'Ní gar ar bith atá déanta agat dom, mar sin, mar fágadh cead a gcinn ag fir Éireann i rith an ama sin.'

'Níorbh amhlaidh é,' arsa Lugh, 'mar tháinig buíon óg mhacra aduaidh ó Eamhain Mhacha. Rinne céad go leith acu ionsaí faoi thrí ar fhir Éireann. Mharaigh siad a thrí oiread dá líon féin ach sa deireadh maraíodh iad féin uilig. Bhí Follamhain, mac Chonchúir, ar throid tú leis ar do chéad lá ag Eamhain Mhacha, ina cheannaire orthu. Mhaígh sé nach rachadh sé abhaile gan chloigeann Ailealla leis agus an choróin óir air. Beirt mhac altrama le hAilill a fuair an ceann is fearr air agus maraíodh é.'

'Is mór mo náire,' arsa Cúchulainn, 'mar, mura mbeinn i mo chodladh, ní dhéanfaí scrios orthu agus ní bheadh mac Chonchúir marbh.'

'Ná bí do do chrá féin, a Chú chaoin,' arsa Lugh, 'níl aon locht ortsa.'

'Fan agam anocht,' arsa an Cú le Lugh Lámhfhada ansin, 'agus bainfidh muid éiric amach ar bhás an mhacra.'

'Ní fhanfaidh leoga,' ar seisean, 'ach imir thusa an cluiche seo go dtí an deireadh anois le fir Éireann, mar ní acusan atá an chumhacht ar do shaol faoi láthair.'

Laoch na Laochra - Scéal Chúchulainn (2015) Gael Linn www.gael-linn.ie

The Boy Corps of Eamhain Mhacha

Réamonn Ó Ciaráin

Boy Corps came south from Eamhain Mhacha.

In the morning Laogh saw a man coming towards them from the north-east.

'A man approaches my little Hound, a tall handsome man with a powerful aura. He wears a green tunic that is fastened with a silver brooch and a silk shirt with embroidery of red gold falling down to his knees. He carries a black shield with a white bronze rim and a five-pronged spear in his other hand. What is most surprising, however, is that nobody in the camp of the Fir Éireann sees this man.'

'If it is so,' said Cúchulainn, 'that the Fir Éireann cannot see him, well I know who it is: a guardian of mine from the otherworld who is coming to help me, for he knows well how difficult it has been to stand alone against the four provinces.'

Lugh Lámhfhada had come from the otherworldly host to speak with Cúchulainn, for he knew that he was exhausted from fighting and lack of sleep.

'Sleep now, my brave Hound,' he said, 'by the grave of Learga, and I will keep a good watch over you for three days and three nights.'

Cúchulainn slipped off into a drowning wave of sleep by the grave of Learga.

This was not surprising, for he had been fighting the host since the feast of Samhain without sleep, bar a few minutes here and there, using the support of his spear with his head on his hands and the spear on his knee. As he slept soundly, Lugh applied magic herbs to his wounds and they all healed. After he had slept for three days and three nights, Cúchulainn woke up and rubbed his face. He was charged with energy and courage once more. He became hungry and craved the closeness of a woman.

'How long was I asleep?' he asked.

'Three days and three nights.'

It was taboo for the people of Ulster to wake Cúchulainn ever since he was a child at Dundalk.

'It is no favour that you have done for me then, for the Fir Éireann have had their way for that time.'

'Not so,' said Lugh, 'for the brave Boy Corps came south from Eamhain Mhacha and a hundred and fifty of them attacked the Fir Éireann three times. They killed three times their own number, but in the end they too were all killed. Follomhain, son of Conchúr, whom you fought on your first day at Eamhain Mhacha, was their leader; he pledged not to return north without Ailill's head complete with its gold crown. Two foster sons of Ailill it was who eventually subdued and killed him.'

'Great is my shame,' said Cúchulainn, 'for had I not been asleep these boys would not have been slaughtered, and neither would Conchúr's son be dead.'

'Do not torment yourself, my gentle Hound,' said Lugh, 'for you are not to blame.'

'Stay with me tonight,' said the Hound, 'and we will take revenge for the slaying of the Boy Corps of Eamhain Mhacha.'

'I shall not stay,' said Lugh, 'but you must play out this game with the Fir Éireann to the end, for your life is in your own hands now.'

Section from *Cúchulainn - Ulster's Greatest Hero* by Réamonn Ó Ciaráin, published by Gael Linn www.gael-linn.ie

Box Room

Maureen Boyle

Returning from Europe on the ferry in a fog I feel like we are in an old fifties movie – all blacks and greys. We take the train from Dover up to London avoiding the question of a dismembered house south of the river and the raw fact that when we reach the city we will part and go to two different rooms – you to a student hall going back to study - me to a basement flat on the edge of Hampstead Heath.

I arrive in a room so full of cardboard boxes I can see little else and everything I own is in them. I have seen this room only once before. It smells a little damp. It is very dark. It is below the level of the street. The owner of the flat sleeps on the other side of the wall. I know where nothing is. I know that I must lie down and sleep in this new bed. I know I will wake up and not know where I am. I know I will have new dreams. I know I will have to get up and go to work in the morning from this new place. I know I will have to learn a new phone number. I know I will have to buy food for myself and cook it. I know that I will have to live the next day and the next outside anyone's gaze. I know I will think of what you are doing almost every minute of every day. I know that I can still smell you and hear your voice. I know that I must not call you. I know it is OK to be afraid. I know it is OK to cry. I know that some day I'll be happy again. I tell myself this.

Often in September I remember that time and the gingkoes in Russell Square where I'd have toast and tea before work in the bright blue London mornings. I was working in the Periodicals Room of Senate House – fetching journals from the tower, making minute entries in the records in ink, finding camaraderie among the other young people amid an old-fashioned and very eccentric English library.

We had been living together for over a year when we decided to make a trip to your past in Strasbourg on a train with wine-coloured leather seats. As a teenager years before you had joined a French order of missionary priests 'The White Fathers' and had trained there. Our trip was a mistake. We were coming to an end and when we got there you began to break up, to break open. The city was postcard perfect – the wooden houses with their ornate scrolled lintels – the little hotel we first stayed in like an inn in Dickens, our first night eating Alsatian flan and my first taste of Gewürztraminer from the Route du Vin. But then we went to stay with your friend – another ex- priest who had settled there - and you sat up with him all night crying. In the morning his French wife drove you to the doctor's – her tanned long legs in the driving seat of the Peugeot, perfect in a wrap dress. She made plum tarts for her pretty children who ran in from school. Why was I there? It was a mistake.

And so we came back and parted and for the rest of the winter I will slowly unpack the boxes and find a place for everything in that single room. I will read Anne Stevenson's bitter biography of Plath in a rocking chair. I will listen for news of you from friends. I will walk down the hill to work past the wolves in the zoo. I will re-read all of the Anne of Green Gables books in a week of flu. I will walk on the Heath on Sundays and eat cakes in Louis's. I will sleep out a snow day. I will try to sound cheerful when I speak to my mother on the phone. I will knit all of the loss into a Donegal tweed jumper heavy enough to take it and wait for spring and your inevitable February letter asking me to try again.

Previously published in *Happy Browsing - An Anthology in Praise of Bookfinders*, published by *The Tangerine* in 2018.

I Didn't Feel the Wasp Sting

Karen Mooney

I didn't flinch, I was numbed, I was elsewhere with fear gnawing
away at my insides whilst I held the pride of your mother in my
jutting chin and spoke, with her tongue, of you, to anyone close by:
"that's my brother"

I travelled to watch you compete in the Manx Grand Prix; not my
first experience of road racing but the first where my investment was
all. The first where the skin was stripped to leave emotions raw,
gaping; exposed.

You'd already had an 'accident' before I arrived yet, despite injury,
your soul rose to the challenge. That bloody minded grit we share
creates traction letting us climb from the depths, it lets us look at the
stars from the dunghill; dream and try

Yes, we may fail some-times but not at trying. It has been said that
we're very trying! Getting back up, getting on; have another go. An
upbringing, clothing genes willed in perpetuity determines the
journey whilst we choose the path

The twists, the turns, the hazards, the race; life, in a few laps but not
of a smooth circuit. A bona fide original terrain, presenting challenge
to judgement, tenacity, courage; testing our ability to adapt, change,
survive, fall and adjust.

These laps, excruciating yet exhilarating as I watch the monitor
praying or perhaps pleading with that angel on your shoulder to keep
you safe. Animated, yet frozen with fear, anaesthetized; I didn't feel
the wasp sting

To Wander, Lost

Nina Francus

You never forget the place you've never been.

Mine was Venice. I was nine years old and had a book about five swarthy teenagers who lived under the canals. They were singular neighbours to an abandoned cathedral, whose stones were parched and charred, iridescent with lichen. Shorn window frames sighed with the breeze, and a single tower bore aloft, for spite or show or heaven's sake.

My father had other ideas. He was a mailman by day and an Incan at heart. Maybe that explained my love of religious rubble: Machu Picchu. Dad chewed the words hard, like first bites into sicky-sweet bubblegum. In our living room sat the glowering figure of an unpronounceable god, six inches high and blessed by a one-eyed witch doctor. Dad rubbed the feathery head every day and never got a step closer. His wallet could not withstand the journey.

The dearest member of our household dreamt of gently curving blades and highlighter hair. A land where the sky is kitten-shaped in its off hours, and no one towers over a wheelchair. But his publication rights were limited, and time stifled further volumes. He never saw the neon lights or bullet trains. At seventeen I cleared little Tokyo from the house – comics, posters, a wishful kimono – because our father could not.

The monthly bills stopped, then, and there was money to spare. But it was ugly, ignoble, and Dad wanted it gone. So I furnished a furnace, enrolled in school. For business, and then Italian, a natural, indulgent balm. After all, I had grown up gondola-shaped, rocked in a chrysalis of cut glass and chiaroscuro.

Postcards bolstered the walls of my dorm room, and perhaps my professor could scent the unsent missives. There was a summer program in Rome, and she clipped the brochure neatly to my final exam. A whole month, with weekend trips to Milan, Florence, and Venice.

Dad agreed to pay but insisted I pack the smallest suitcase in the house. Perhaps he predicted the dangers of winged lions and golden spires wound with angels. I suspect he envied the sway of far away, but could no longer bear it himself. Four walls and a roof had once held him in; now they held him up. His shoulders stooped as he helped me pack.

I slept through the flight and dreamed of canals. They were thick, gelatinous rivers I breathed through my ears. I squirmed in my seat until the jolt of wheels on asphalt woke me.

Between classes, I circumambulated. Rome impressed but did not suit me. Everything oozed obsolescence, from the slouching river to the tracts of architectural crumble.

The summer passed. Rome. Milan. Rome. Florence. Rome.

I woke at sunrise that final weekend and sat by the window. Morning splashed the sky as I clutched a weathered children's book. The broken spine split around stained pages, folded corners, and the whiff of happiness.

At 8:00 o'clock, fifty-seven quasi-Italian speakers gathered in the entryway, followed by two professors and a guide. The walk to the train was downhill, and my impatience brimmed over the pavement, scattering loose change and cigarette butts.

At the end of the road, we were greeted by an angry mob. Transportation attendants ringed the station, complete with an arcade of policemen.

Words flew, sharp and loud. Our guide was arguing with a policeman, spluttering something about the train schedule, and dysfunctional *sindicati*. A single word winged over the crowd: *sciopero*.

One professor extracted her phone. With every scroll, her face tightened. This was not, after all, the land of stripes and stars. Strikes did not break out like bar fights. Trains did not dismantle from thirty years of planned negligence. There had to be buses. Shuttles. Rickshaws. Anything.

A uniformed man shouted over the crowd. Two days' strike. Nationwide. Limited regional service only.

The blows fell, ironclad, and I staggered. An army of feather-headed gods could not produce sixty tickets to Venice over an Italian picket line.

Our guide knew as much. He returned to the group, muttering apologies, and began reciting the virtues of Tivoli. Only an hour away. Hadrian's summer home. Better something than nothing.

Blood rushed to my ears and a vivid picture of my calendar slid, sluggish, through my digestive tract. The flight to some overpopulated coastal city. The bus ride home. The extra days I hadn't bought because it was July and a year-old grave needed visiting.

I melted from the crowd, waning through the city. The empty streets were a relief to my pounding heart, but I did not know it. I couldn't feel the pavement or sunlight; the foggy mantle of a night unslept; the tremulous betrayal of a bag already packed.

The last I felt on my long walk to nowhere was the collapse of a paper cathedral. It slipped between my fingers, ink stains and creases intact, to join five swarthy companions in their fast-flowing home.

Christmas Disaster

Doreen McBride

Disaster loomed. Granny and Aunt said they were coming for Christmas. The trouble was we loved both of them and didn't have the guts to say 'No!'

Granny was a keen Presbyterian, a regular churchgoer, who hated what she referred to as 'the demon drink'

Aunt was an alcoholic, who reckoned certain doors should never be darkened. She loved what she referred to as 'a good old booze up' and a lack of alcohol made her fly into a rage.

At a recent family Christening, she'd had a temper tantrum and yelled, 'It's not a proper Christening without a decent drink! That poor baby's head hasn't been properly wet! It's a disgrace!'

We had an emergency family meeting to discuss the situation.

The family decided Granny couldn't reasonably object if we told her we were taking biblical advice and having a little wine for our stomach's sake. If necessary we'd remind her the first miracle Jesus performed was making wine at a wedding feast. As a result, wine, if not taken to excess, can't be wrong.

We thought, with a little intelligent manoeuvring, we could bluff our usual seasonal booze up.

Husband would give Granny brown lemonade instead of the dry sherry we traditionally serve with the soup.

We'd have wine with the main course, forgo using brandy to set the Christmas pudding alight and follow up the meal with an Irish coffee. Granny's coffee would be minus the whiskey while Aunt's would contain her usual triple shot.

The whole idea was a nightmare and husband became an insomniac worrying in case he got the drinks mixed-up.

He did!

All went well until Irish coffee was served.

Granny took a mouthful, swallowed, choked and groaned.

I had a sip.

It nearly blew my head off.

Husband tasted it.

'That's poisonous!' he said, before adding, with great presence of mind, 'Poor Granny. I am so sorry. That's my fault entirely. Please accept my abject apology. I noticed one of the glasses had a stain on its bottom and I put some Fairy liquid in it. The cat distracted me. I must have put your coffee and cream in the glass with the fairy liquid. I'm really sorry. I'll get you another one.'

He escaped into the kitchen.

I followed.

Aunt arrived a second later. 'Here!' she said, 'You must have given me granny's coffee. I wondered what the hell was wrong with it! Don't waste good whiskey by throwing it down the sink. Here! Swop glasses. I'll drink that to get rid of it and you can make me another one!'

'Do you mean to say,' I asked, as she knocked back the offending Irish coffee, 'you got whiskey-free Irish coffee and didn't complain?'

'Yes!' she smiled, 'after all, it's Christmas, the season of goodwill. And I think Granny's guessed what you're up to and she's keeping quiet about it!

Inferno

Rachel Toner

The walls cascade, the entrails blaze in the midst of the
Drummers call. You hear the voice inside your head,
Calling the world to fall.
You hear the crack of the whip on your back
And the backs of all the mortals. Yet you do not stir,
But watch the beast who beats and tears the flesh.
'Deep down below, you will go!' Calls the creature of
Fortune. For down below is where sinners go and here we are
Forsaken.
The Greatest Man who should have saved us with his father's
Plan, has left us here to mourn. From up above we feel no love,
Up there were angels are born.
Oh, we long to make the journey through the stages of this Hell.
Like Dante, pass the ice and fire and the River Styx so well.
But we have no poet to guide us, no gleaming light ahead.
No, here we stay and here we pray, for all
Good in our souls is dead.
Please pity us! And yet do not, for sinners often mourn. It is in a
Sad and rotten heart that the sinner's trait is born.
So think on us, for the fire that burns is born on earth
And it is from earth, we fell.

End of the Line

Omaya Nasser

A bell chimes as the front door to the café opens, but no bell hangs there. The woman entering looks surprised at the sound and shivers. A gust of wind enters with her, dragging a leaf in its wake, which twirls on the floor for a while before settling down in a corner.

The woman sits down at her regular table by the window looking out onto the street, its dark outside and as she looks she can only see her reflection looking back at her, the hat shadowing her eyes and the blood red lipstick shining on her lips. The café is empty except for the barman who brings over a cup of coffee without her asking for it. After this brief interaction, silence, except for the clock that ticks on the wall and the fluorescent tubes flickers.

The woman doesn't touch her cup. She looks into the pool of black coffee as if it would reach out to her and pull her in. She is mesmerized. She holds her breath and then releases it slowly. This helps her ease the iron grasp on her heart, and the blood flows faster through her veins. She has to wait, be patient. She reaches into her bag and pulls out the note that is all creased and stained. It reads:

Meet me at the corner café by the bus stop at eight thirty p.m. Please, don't be late.

E.H

She puts it back into her purse and pours one spoon of sugar into her cup and stirs, the spell is broken, and the coffee is ice cold. She orders another one, this time sugar is poured instantly and she takes a sip of the hot coffee, she puts the cup down and rummages through her bag. She finds her book, takes it out, opens the first page and reads the first line;

A bell chimes as the front door to the café opens …

72

The woman looks up and there he is. A ghost of the man that he used to be, but it's him, he's come for her. She gets up and rushes to him, they embrace and walk out the door.

A bell chimes, the door is open and a leaf is dancing in a gust of wind. The barman looks up and sees the woman slumped over the table. He walks over to her, feels her pulse. The wait is over.

Incunabula III

Maureen Boyle

i.m. Pat Boyle 1930-2008

He bought that house from a jilted Orangeman
who didn't know that land was not to be sold to Fenians
and tried to buy it back. Maggie Henderson
was Orange enough to make up for us – King Billy
looming in her hall and tea brewed for the 'wee soldiers'
who set up checkpoints on the road. Her quiet husband Hughie
walked with the Black Men in August. She kept cats
that reeked and snoozed on the roof of her henhouse.
They said there were dead Franciscans under us –
a medieval graveyard but all we ever found were shards
of willow pattern when we tried to dig to China
and the monastery overgrown at the turn of the river
where we went to play in the sheep tunnels under the railway lines.
The Mc Cullaghs were our neighbours on the other side
who arrived bedraggled one night in a storm
when the electricity off. They came from the mountains –
'the Plum'. She had a countrywoman's disdain for pets
and drowned the only kitten I ever owned.
I would sing on my swing and imagine
that Paris lay beyond the hills.

From *The Work of a Winter* as published in 2018 by Arlen House Press.

Extract from 'Kirsty's Vow'

Patricia Hanlon

I want to talk to you both about my married name. It's been playing on my mind,' Kirsty hesitated. 'I've been thinking about how I like Kirsty Malone – it's always had a great ring to it, hasn't it?'

Rose turned the volume down on the television and Tommy set down his newspaper.

'Kate once told me my name was the first thing she liked about me, before she'd even met me! Did you know that?' Kirsty crossed and uncrossed her legs.

Her parents said nothing, so she went on.

'So, I'm starting to think I'd rather stay Kirsty Malone. Or, maybe do the double-barreled thing, you know – "Kirsty Hall-Malone, or Malone-Hall." What do you think?' Kirsty kicked off her shoes and curled her legs up under her on the chair.

'Sounds fair enough to me, love,' Tommy Malone lifted his newspaper again. 'Sure, anything goes these days.'

'Thomas! Think about what you're saying!' Rose lifted her feet off the stool and pushed it away from her with one toe.

'What's the big deal, mum?' Kirsty got up, lifted the abandoned footstool, and brought it over to where she sat. She settled herself back in the armchair and propped her feet up.

'Kirsty, it's preposterous! While Ted isn't exactly the ideal suitor I'd have chosen for *my* daughter, the Halls are a well-respected family. You can't snub them!'

'I wouldn't be snubbing anyone!' Kirsty looked at the television; the cookery programme was about to start.

'Kirsty.' Rose Malone's voice was calmer. 'Isobel Hall is in my Women's Institute and, while we don't socialise in the same 'circles,' - Rose's mimed inverted commas were a bit more like rabbits' ears – 'I certainly cannot risk her taking any offence. She's tipped to be President next year.' Rose nodded her wide-eyed head reverently.

'I didn't know Isobel dabbled in politics,' Kirsty's dad winked over at her.

'President of the *W.I.*, Tommy,' Rose said with an exasperated sigh.

Kirsty grinned at her dad. Her mum was so easy to wind up.

'No, Kirsty. Absolutely not. I won't have my only daughter, who I've tried to raise as a lady, acting like some bra-burning feminist and taking a double-barreled name. Or worse - keeping your maiden name.' Rose looked imploringly at her daughter.

'What's wrong with her maiden name? I like the idea of Kirsty keeping *my* family name,' Tommy tried.

'I'm sure you do, Tommy. I'm sure you do.' Rose stood up. 'I'm going to watch that cookery programme in the kitchen, in peace. Kirsty, please drop the idea. For *my* sake.' And with that, Rose exited the room.

'You'd better let her win this one, pet,' said Tommy from behind his newspaper.

Kirsty smiled. Kirsty wasn't particularly close to her dad; he was a man of few words. But sometimes Kirsty's dad could say more in one sentence than her mum could in one day. Kirsty admitted to herself that she didn't feel strongly about changing her name anyway; it was just something that had started to niggle at her. But Kirsty's dad was right – she'd let it go.

'Where's the man himself tonight, anyway?' The newspaper rustled as Tommy turned a page.

'Who?' Kirsty reached down for the IPad.

'Ted? How come you're not out with him tonight?'

'Oh, Ted's out with Charlie tonight, dad. They're away playing pool. He wants to enjoy his last Saturday nights out before he becomes a mutt, as Kate would put it.'

Tommy folded his newspaper and looked at his daughter. 'A mutt?'

'It stands for Man Under the Thumb.'

Kirsty's dad threw back his head and laughed louder and longer than Kirsty had seen him do in years.

'That's priceless. Where does she get them?'

'Aw, you know Kate. Maybe it's the English teacher in her.'

'There aren't too many mutts around nowadays,' Tommy mused.

Jonah and the Whale

Gaynor Kane

He arrived at the coast on autopilot, memories of last night
burning a hole in his head. A feeling of dread crept up from his toes.
Fists in pockets against the November chill,
from the dunes he looked down on the spectacle below.
He knew the bible story, it resonated through his body like a
heartbeat.
Jonah imagined himself in a past life, his skinny form,
inside the mountainous bulk of washed-up whale.

Sticky, tar coloured, bigger than a capsized fishing boat, the heap
of stiff Sperm Whale dripped stench into sand. Sand dunes shifted
as if the whale's decay was infectious, dark veins permeated the
beach,
grasses turning brown. Circling, swooping Seagulls imitated Vulture
cousins.
He listened to a rhythmic breeze pulsing across the coast
like ghostly breathing of a solid swimmer grounded; imagined he
could hear
short snips of slimy sinews snapping, muscle melting, skin splitting.

Rumours rippled throughout transfixed onlookers; there was talk of a
burial
but the beach was not deep enough to inter the mammoth sea-
mammal.
Then the hard hats of the State Highways Division arrived
dragging threatening clouds from Route 101. They frowned, pinched
nostrils, scratches bald heads, did calculations, periodically sticking
pencils
behind their ears, trying to give the impression of making plans

but Jonah could see in their eyes they were clueless, stumped,
fish out of water.

They hypothesised 8 tonnes of dead whale divided by half a tonne
of dynamite was the right ratio to blast blubber to bits. Twenty cases
of TNT
carried like a funeral procession across the beach and buried.

Jonah was asked to move further back. A quarter of a mile
should be a safe distance.

The Highways Chief crossed himself then laid hands on the
detonator.

This was a sign, Jonah bowed his head,
he was sorry, please God show forgiveness.

Jonah felt the crowd gasp then hold their breath,
he held his breath.

Wind dropped.
Ghost breath stopped.

Grasses stilled.

Seagulls scarpered.

Silence.

An Chéad Mharú

Réamonn Ó Ciaráin

Bhí an chéad mharú déanta ag Cúchulainn i gcoinne naimhde móra na Craoibhe Rua. Ar an bhealach ar ais, thángthas ar thréad fianna agus shíl Cúchulainn go mbeadh sé iontach ceann acu sin a thabhairt ar ais go hEamhain Mhacha leis. D'iarr sé ar Laogh dul níos cóngaraí. Léim sé amach as an charbad agus rith ina ndiaidh. Rug sé greim ar fhia fireann agus cheangail le cúl an charbaid é. Chonaic sé ealta ealaí ansin agus shocraigh stangadh a bhaint as cuid acu lena chrann tabhaill. Thóg sé anuas breis agus scór éan ina mbeatha agus cheangail le fráma an charbaid iad, le téad ar leith d'achan éan. Mar seo a chuaigh siad i dtreo Eamhain Mhacha, na héin ar eitilt os a gcionn, an fia ag rith ina ndiaidh agus cloigne chlann Neachtain ag bogadach ar thaobh an charbaid.

Bhí riastradh millteanach feirge agus fuinnimh ar an laoch óg le corraí na troda agus na seilge.

Chonaic Leabharcham agus na mná eile ag Eamhain Mhacha an radharc iontach seo ag teacht ionsorthu agus tháinig eagla a mbáis orthu. Shíl siad go mbeadh gach mac máthar i gcontúirt, mura gcuirfí suaimhneas ar Chúchulainn. Shocraigh siad dul amach agus iad nocht ó bhun go barr le Cúchulainn óg a phreabadh amach as an riastradh. Nuair a chonaic Cúchulainn na mná nochta go léir os a chomhair, tháinig náire air agus mhaolaigh cuid den alltacht a bhí air. Chuir siad isteach i ndabhcha uisce é ach phléasc an chéad cheann le teas a choirp, chuaigh an dara ceann ina ghal ach sa deireadh tháinig suaimhneas ar Chúchulainn sa tríú ceann. Thug na mná faoi deara go raibh seacht méar ar an dá lámh ag Cúchulainn agus seacht ladhar ar a dhá chos. Bhí seacht n-imreasc ina shúile, ceithre cinn i súil amháin agus trí cinn sa tsúil eile agus bhí sé camshúileach i súil amháin. Bhí trí dhath éagsúla ar a chuid gruaige agus bhí ceithre loigín ina dhá leiceann. Agus bhí solas an churaidh ag lonrú óna cheann.

Cé go raibh clú mór ar Chúchulainn i measc mhná Eamhain Mhacha, deirtí go raibh trí locht air; go raibh sé ró-óg, ró-dhána agus ró-álainn. Ina ainneoin sin, áit ar bith a mbíodh laochra ó shin i leith, chantaí molta Chúchulainn agus bhí grá ag fir, ag mná, ag ríthe agus ag saoithe dó. Bhí a fhios ag achan duine ón rí anuas go ndéanfadh an laoch seo mórán gaiscí ar son Uladh amach anseo.

Laoch na Laochra - Scéal Chúchulainn (2015) Gael Linn www.gael-linn.ie

Yeats

Christopher Moore

Am I a fraud?

I sometimes think I must be. I wander these paths, these woods at Coole, this tranquil refuge from the cares of life, so many times, so many days, with none but my own thoughts for company, and I lose myself so deeply in my own imaginings, my own dreams, my own image of the world and my life as I would like it to be, that these thoughts, these dreams take on a life that seems to make them real. I find myself passing by the lake, peering at the lonely man staring up from the unspoilt surface of the water, disappearing into incoherent ripples as the swans come in to land, and the whole mirror before me is broken and disturbed, and for a moment, it's like I receive an epiphany. A moment of perfect, unkind clarity, where I see just how alone I have made myself- on these walks, in this seclusion. How hermetic, how reclusive, how hidden away from the truths of life I have allowed myself to become. And the dreams, in that instant, seem foolish.

Because she *has* refused me. More than once now. Has been graceful, has been kind, has been charitable about it, has remained in my company and on at least the periphery of my life, but she will never be mine. If her inclinations towards me had anything approaching the strength of mine towards her, it would not require more than one attempt to convince her to accept me. Nothing had changed, for her part at least, between the first and second asking. So, I have no right, there is no logic, in expecting that a third or fourth entreaty would result in a different outcome. She has made her feelings, however kindly or graciously, perfectly clear. This is a one-sided infatuation, no matter how strong. And deep, deep within, when examining the honest truth in my heart, I know this is not going to change.

So, then, does that make the rest of my life, my leanings, my outlook, fraudulent? Does my interest in, my being drawn towards, that revolutionary spirit she so passionately embodies, stem solely from my love for her person? If she were not leading, not advocating, not striving for her political purpose, would I feel that purpose compel me as fiercely? Am I not, in truth, seduced to its purpose, to the zeal of its followers, merely because of her?

This does bother me. Of course it bothers me. It would affect anyone's conscience, if they stood and thought about it for long enough- a possible untruth at the core of their very being, their very life, their very worldview. If one had the time and the space to stand and think about it.

But, the truth- the enduring, powerful, perhaps pathetic truth- is that I do not have that time, and that space. For as I stand here, by this water, by these magnificent creatures, with all the freedom to contemplate that any man could reasonably ask for, all I can continue to think about it how my soul aches for her. How I long for her with every waking moment and breath. It has been a gift from Heaven for my writing, for my work. As an artist, I can have no complaint about the inspiration she has afforded me.

But, as a man, as a human being, as an aching soul... I fear it is an emptiness that will never be filled.

And Then She Danced

Jay Faulkner

Personal space was a distant memory as everyone huddled together despite the fetid smells. People languished in their own filth which stained clothing and floor alike. Three days inside the train, without food or water, had taken its toll. Low moans of despair were drowned out by the cacophony of metal on metal as the miles of track were eaten up.

The daily change in light, glimpsed through gaps in panelled walls, marked the passage of time since leaving Westerbork. Then they'd kept apart, families protective of each other, fearful of everyone else; now brought together by the insults sewn roughly onto their clothing.

And amongst them, one man stayed separate. An oasis in the desert of bodies. Watching. Ignoring; never ignored.

He opened a packet from within his pocket. The noise ripped through the silence. No-one moved. He took out cheese and savoured a small bite. His second bite was stopped as, from within the press of bodies, a small form moved towards him.

'What's that?' The young girl asked, eyes wide, cheeks sunken hollows. Her hands clutched a pink bundle against her grime-stained dress.

'It's cheese,' he answered sharply, looking around the sea of faces, relaxing when he saw no-one else had moved. 'It's *my* cheese.'

'Can I have some?' She unconsciously reached out a small, dirty hand towards him. Her bundle slipped, falling until the laces of ballet shoes tied around her wrist halted the drop.

'Are they yours?' he gestured with the cheese towards the shoes.

'Papa said I could take them with me,' she answered with the shadow of a smile. 'They're my favourite.'

'You dance?'

'Every evening, before my prayers, I practice.'

'That is a good girl,' he nodded. 'My daughter likes ... liked ... to dance, too.'

'Where is she?'

His face fell into deeper shadows. 'She is gone, little one.'

'I can't find my Papa,' she said softly, looking around the still forms in the wagon. 'Some of them say he's on a different train ...'

'Don't worry, then,' he stared at her; his face still. 'You'll see him soon.'

'I'm hungry.'

'We all are, child,' he said, then held the cheese towards her. 'But, if you dance for me, if you show me what your lessons taught you, then you will have this as a reward.'

Without a word, she sat and pulled the small shoes onto her filthy feet. The train swayed, wood creaking, metal grinding; moonlight streamed, sending slivers of light weaving around the shadows. Laces were tied tightly around her ankles before she stood again.

And then she danced.

Gaunt arms rose, sweeping in front of her with movements that were hesitant at first but, as music that only she could hear, became graceful and assured. She dropped into a low plié before rising up and turned a slow, measured circle. The pirouette finished and she paused, taking a breath, extended her arms towards the man as her body seemed to lift itself; toes took her so meagre weight, calf muscles straining, insteps curving, and she became en pointé. Her body stilled, then stopped completely and, for a perfect moment, she stood there; the ballerina she could become clearly seen.

The train juddered and, she fell; the moment lost.

She readjusted her dress; one small hand toyed with the yellow star sewn across her heart. The man looked away, his hand mimicking her movement. He traced the swastika on his arm. Without a word he held out the cheese then watched as she snatched it, vanishing into the press of bodies as the train shuddered to a stop. A murmur from outside got louder. The door was pulled open. The man scurried to one side as voices shouted, demanding everyone move to the platform. When they didn't - couldn't - move fast enough hard-eyed men from outside started pulling and shoving until, finally, the carriage was empty; leaving only the man. He stared at the hard-eyed men who nodded back then started pushing the people away from the train; into the night.

Wiping crumbs of cheese with one hand down his trousers, the other hand on the rifle that had never left his grasp, he left the wagon. As he jumped down he saw a flash of colour back inside and saw the ballet shoes lying alone; forgotten. He moved to retrieve them, for the girl, but, as the moonlight reflected off the sign on the platform, 'Auschwitz', he simply closed the door.

She wouldn't need them.

KiltyRelics

Trish Bennett

In the eighties,
far out relations breezed in our door,
to trace their roots
and 'ooh' and 'aah' our home,
one hundred and fifty years old — a museum,
my brother and I on display;
'Twentieth century Irish Teens'.
Mam stuffed them with tae, tart and treacle bread,
'Go on, go on, a little bit more',
while Dad dished out hot ones and stories galore.
Later, he drove down dung filled roads,
made them stop, to let fairies cross.
They hopped out with flashes,
white innocent smiles,
and pressed roses from hedges
in their Ireland guides.

In the graveyard by Lough Melvin's shore,
Dad had no clue where the ancestors lay,
a minor point, they'd come all this way.
He showed them a grave by the limestone wall,
question after question came,
until they asked,
'Why the unmarked plot?'
His answer nailed the questions shut.
When people left long ago,
t'was tradition to send money home,
for a decent wake
and a good headstone'.

They called to a cottage on the return,
a mound of stones in the field beside,
was all that remained of their ancestors lives.

My Father, spoke to the man at the door,
'They've come from the states, we can't disappoint',
so the man became a far out cousin,
threw himself into the role,
'Come in, come into my home.
Your Great Grandmothers bed's in the lower room,
where she knelt every night to say her prayers,
she sat here, at the hearth
— sit down — sit down in her chair'.
He gave them a piece of the hearthstone
— a relic to share.

The far out relations
breezed home
with tears in their eyes,
and rose tinted pages
in their Ireland Guides.

Kilty Relics was awarded 'The Leitrim Guardian Literary Award for Poetry' and published
in its 2018 edition.

Revisiting

Elaine Toal

I felt the cold air seep into my bones as I stood beside my car, its heat fading. From across the road, I looked at the home we once shared. I wanted to scoff, the Christmas lights were up, 'It's still bloody November' I muttered. He's become one of 'those people' I thought smugly, before reining myself in. I was not here for confrontation.

I started across the road towards the gaudy flashing lights. Taking off a glove, I gave a firm rap on the door. I had long given up ringing door bells. They never work.

A sliver of light widened into the hall as a door opened and a figure moved towards me. I felt my heartbeat quicken as the adrenaline entered my veins ahead of what I had mentally billed as 'the big reunion'.

The door opened. He loomed large in the doorframe, almost filling its height. The light behind him caught a dusting of grey in his hair that wasn't there before.

He said nothing, reaching back inside to turn on the light overhead. The bare bulb was blinding to my night adjusted eyes. I blinked and attempted a smile. He did not return it.

'I thought the last time you closed this door was the end of this. But here you are.' He said softly so as not to cause a scene. I didn't speak. He seemed composed. When I imagined how this would go, his eyes filled with tears and he put his arms out to me. But tonight, on the porch, his eyes were hard and cold. The warmth that I remembered was no longer there. Did I do this to him?

'Are you afraid of being on your own at Christmas? You come knocking at my door to see if there's any room at the inn?' He spat the words at me. I felt myself flinch. He had landed the first blow and I saw that he liked that. Emboldened, he continued, 'If you are looking for your things, you're too late. They went in the skip years ago. I thought about sending them on, but you made sure I wouldn't find you.'

This much was true. I left without a trace. I just got in my car and I drove. Miles and miles through the darkness, my jaw set, not allowing the tears to fall. I knew if they started they would never stop, that all the years wasted together, would come pouring out, a salty river of grief for time lived and lost.

He was waiting for me to speak. But now that I was here I didn't know what to say. His attitude had wiped the apology from my lips. I imagined I would tell him I was sorry. Sorry that I didn't trust him, that my jealous nature had driven a wedge between us and now in hindsight, I could see how wrong I was. I had thrown many accusations at him. That he was being unfaithful to me, that I loved him more than he loved me. There was no proof of infidelity, only a jealous nature and a stinging vocabulary designed to hurt. There were many fights but the last one was the worst. It was a vicious screaming row that lasted long into the night. We threw words at one another, launched like hand grenades intent on inflicting maximum damage. I was good at that, filling my words with poison and scorn. That time he did not retaliate, he just stood there and let the words rain down around him. That's how I knew it was the end. He had no more fight left.

I wanted him to know that I had changed, that I was in control of my emotions now, that my younger self would be proud. Before I could compose myself and utter anything, the door behind him opened and a smaller figure appeared. He whirled around, blocking the door, mumbling a few words to pacify the enquirer. But he wasn't quick enough. I saw enough to know that it was her.

Then, under the stark light of the porch that was once the entrance to our home, I straightened myself up. I turned on my heel without a word. After all, what was left to say?

As I settled back into the warmth of my car I was glad that the tears for him were unshed; the tears I shed now were for me.

First published in *Circling Round Conformity,* published in 2018 by Dunfanaghy Writers' Circle and edited by Alf McCreary.

Bás Chúchulainn

Réamonn Ó Ciaráin

'Tóg leat anois cloigeann an Chú, a Chinn Bhearraide,' arsa Conall, 'le go mbeidh sé ag Eimhear.'

'Tógfaidh cinnte,' arsa Ceann Bhearraide, 'mar is tábhachtaí liom an ceann uasal seo a chur sa talamh ná baint a bheith agam le slad an díoltais.'

Nigh sé ceann an Chú agus thóg ar ais go Dún Dealgan agus chuir isteach i lámha a mhná chéile, Eimhear, é. Chuir Eimhear ar ais ar an mhuineál é go cúramach. I ndiaidh tamaill, thóg sí an ceann in aice lena brollach agus chaoin bás an laoich fá chroí dubh. Shúigh sí a liopaí gorma agus d'ól a chuid fola fuaire. Ansin chuir sí caille sróil thar a cheann.

'Mo bhrón is mo mhilleadh,' arsa Eimhear, 'nach uasal an chuma atá ar an cheann seo inniu agus nach iomaí iníon rí agus taoisigh ar fud na cruinne a bheadh ag tabhairt ómóis, dá mbeadh a fhios acu é a bheith sínte. Scoth na bhfear in Éirinn agus in Albain, ba tú grá fhir an domhain mhóir agus is mór mo bhris a bheith anseo ar Mhachaire Mhuirtheimhne i do dhiaidh. Ní raibh bean phósta ná dhíomhaoin in Éirinn ná in Albain ná ar dhroim an domhain nach raibh in éad liom, in éad liom go dtí inniu.'

Rug sí greim ar a chuid lámh agus ghearr isteach ina chuid feola lena hingne.

'Is mór líon na ríthe, na taoisigh agus na laochra a thit ar mhachaire an chatha ag na lámha láidre seo agus is mór an líon éan agus ainmhí fiánta a thit le do scil i mbun seilge. Is mór an stór agus taisce a bronnadh ort ag filí agus ag saoithe na cruinne....................

'Agus ar fhág Cúchulainn teachtaireacht ná treoir domsa sular éag sé, a Laoigh?'

'Níor fhág, a Eimhear, ach le rá nach raibh tú le dul le haon fhear murar Ultach é.'

'Furasta é sin a dhéanamh,' arsa Eimhear, 'mar ní bheidh fear ar bith eile de na fir uilig ar an domhan seo i ndiaidh mo Chúchulainn.'

Laoch na Laochra - Scéal Chúchulainn (2015) Gael Linn www.gael-linn.ie

The Realisation

Jude Alexzander

No one single thing had caused the Realisation. Like the rest of his life, no dramatic events led up to it; rather it was as the dripping of a tap. Soft. Unnoticed. Mundane. Barely audible amid the monotonous clamour of everyday routine.

Drip. It was just a smile, a laugh. A cheeky comment here and there, and the habitual smack on the arm that followed.

Drip. Gradually seeping through the cracks to pool innocently at the bottom of his consciousness.

Friends. Colleagues. Lads. Football banter. Heads bending close together over the desk to plot against their *pompous arse* of a supervisor. It was commiserations, congratulations and a quiet bit of good advice when one or the other was too close to taking a customer's head off. It was sympathy and practical jokes on sleepy, hung-over Saturday mornings when nobody in their right minds should be calling Tech Support.

The tittering jibes of their colleagues had been dismissed without a thought. Silly shower of bastards, he told himself. They were so starved for excitement in this godforsaken place, they'd latch onto anything.

Drip. Nothing to be aware of, until chill comprehension finally soaked through. Everything has a saturation point.

One dreary Friday evening, after all their macho-talk, the other flaky buggers from Team 4 hadn't shown up for the customary 'lads' drinks after work. Suddenly it was just the two of them, idling the evening away amongst the cheap lights and cheap pints. Two friends sitting alone in a sea of people, setting the world to rights, complaining about work (the supervisor really was an arse.) Talking about everything and nothing at all.

93

Drip. That smile at some bitchy comment he'd made. The peals of hysterical laughter that left them both wheezing and breathless over something so *foolish* that he'd never be able to remember later. A hand casually ruffling his hair. The lazy pressure of a knee against his thigh as they shuffled over to let some reeling punters past.

The tilt of that throat in the gaudy flicker of the games machines, all highlights and hollows and five-o-clock shadow. The Adam's apple working as he drained his pint. He caught himself staring and forced his eyes away.

Drip. Saturation point. Realisation. Perhaps the teasing hadn't been so far from the mark after all. His chest ached. Two friends? Two blind idiots who couldn't see what everyone else could, in the end

The walk home was quiet and bittersweet. Sometimes their arms bumped gently as they crunched along the icy pavement to the taxi rank- the longest and shortest street in creation

One last hug. A strong grip on his shoulder, lingering for just a moment. That wonderful smile again, gentle now under the muted glow of the streetlights.

Then it was over. He did not ask to share the cab and all too soon he was standing alone.

Snowflakes fell as cold, damp kisses on his tired face. Eventually, he turned towards home.

The Realisation was published in *The Blue Nib* magazine in December 2019

The Night Before Christmas was Cool

Eddie McClenaghan

'Twas the night before Christmas, when all through the hamlet,
Festive movies were streaming on TVs and tablets.
The gleam of the houses decorated with lights,
Signalled to Santa to stop here on his flight.

The WiFi was off and the children in bed,
Dreaming of presents and turkey they'd be fed.
I turned on the heating to warm up the house,
At the request of my shivering spouse.

When out the front I heard such a buzz and a whirring,
I peered through the blinds to see what was occurring.
A swarm of green and red drones were hovering around,
With one in my garden that must've crashed down.

A slim figured man with a well-groomed white beard,
Wearing red skinny jeans and woolly red hat appeared.
He was making a call and his patience looked short,
I heard on his loudspeaker 'This is Elfdesk support'.
The grounded drone missed the latest update,
For added components to carry more weight.
Santa took out his tablet and logged on to Elfdesk,
And followed instructions for a Santa drone health check.

'Tap Dashboard, Tap Answers and type in my question…
Are there spare drones in the area? – End of support session.'
His support call dropped and he lost his connection,
He needed help to get things back in the right direction.

I opened the window and gave Santa a lifeline,
I whispered to him 'Come in, use our WiFi!'
He took the drone and the presents and climbed in through the window,
So he could come into the warm house and get a better signal.

We had left him some cookies and a pint of real ale,
But Santa preferred some juiced avocado and kale.
The other drones had delivered the presents in the hamlet,
While Santa searched for a spare one on his green and red tablet.

He wore a red and white plaid shirt with red trouser braces,
Red and white canvas trainers with candy cane coloured laces.
He was taller and thinner than what my parents told me,
With thick framed glasses as gold as could be.

There was no spare drones available, all were in use,
He scratched his beard in thought as he finished his juice.
I had an idea that just popped in my head,
Then I invited Santa out to my garden shed.

My remote control helicopter had seen better days,
Though shining in the moonlight was the black propeller blade.
It was a little too small to fit on the drone,
So we continued our search with the torch on my phone.

I spotted something that might fit the bill,
I wondered 'Could it?' and Santa said 'It will!'
An old white desk fan with large blades and motor,
Plenty of power and a makeshift rotor.

Me and Santa worked at fixing the drone,
Getting it ready for his next drop zone.
It was a bit odd looking but it was up in the air
and able to carry a garden deck chair!

Santa was grateful for the help he received,

A magical fellow you better believe!
He placed our presents all under the tree,
Beautifully wrapped for my family and me.

He hopped back in his sleigh clicking his finger at the drones,
They whirred into action for another present drop zone.
I heard him call out as he flew to great height,
'May your Christmas be merry, be cool and be white!'

The Dead Counter

Paul Anthony

P James O'Meara rises from a routinely dreamless sleep and switches off the alarm at six twenty seven am just before it has a chance to wake Miriam, his wife of forty one and a half years and……. two weeks. He kisses her lightly on the cheek and goes to the *en suite*. It is no different from any other morning: a cold water shave with his Wilkinson's Sword Single Blade (he rejoices in the fact that Miriam can still source them on '*that e bay thing*'), a splash of Old Spice, teeth are cleaned once in a clockwise motion, then twice anti clockwise with Pepsodent, then a rinse with Listerine…… Original Flavour of course.

He checks his moustache. It is not Monday so it is not time for a trim but it looks a trifle unruly which it had not been on the previous night's inspection. He dithers. A quick selective pluck with the tweezers or a more all embracing cut with the nail scissors? He decides that he must look his best for his clients so he chooses the former and rinses the offending two hairs down the sink with the panache of a boxer dispatching his opponent to the canvas.

He selects a white shirt from the six others in his walk in wardrobe…..Miriam has her own…. and a red tie to go with it. He dons his black non iron trousers with grey braces, and puts on his horribly contrasting green cardigan, brown tweed jacket, and brown brogue shoes with steel heel tips both worn down on the right hand side.

A final check of the bedroom, and he creeps downstairs. The heel tips echo like those of a prison warder on the tiles of the kitchen. His cranberry juice and prunes are waiting for him in the fridge. He likes to be regular. Regular is good! They are prepared the previous night….by Miriam. It cuts two minutes and twenty seconds off his morning routine. He fills the kettle just enough for his one cup of tea,

Tetley of course….leaves not bags…, and places a single piece of Brennan's Batch Bread in the toaster. He spreads the latter with Golden Cow and nibbles. He drinks the tea noiselessly then takes his clipboard from behind the biscuit tin.

Having checked the list, he needlessly licks his pencil stub and enters the new date at the top. He will sign the bottom later.

He checks the order of the day. It is indeed in order. Order is good. He opens the front door. A glorious early sun invites him to embrace the summer, but before he accepts, he takes his haversack, packs his clipboard, his pre prepared lunch (another five minutes and twenty seconds saved) *and* his umbrella, just in case. One can never be too sure with modern weather forecasting.

He cleans his teeth for the second time in the downstairs toilet and closes the door behind him. It is six fifty seven precisely, two minutes ahead of the previous day. It puzzles him as he has done nothing differently and vows to review his routine with his eleven o'clock hot milk and sweet digestive biscuit.

He goes to the shed and retrieves his green Raleigh bicycle with the three speed Sturmey Archer gears….. three gears are plenty for anybody….. puts on the bicycle clips and does a running start, mounting as a cowboy would do with a galloping horse.

The journey takes thirteen minutes precisely. He parks his bike, locks it to his usual lamp post and retrieves the bunch of keys from his haversack.

Primrose Grove Sheltered Housing is always his first port of call. Each of the ten buildings has four separate dwellings. If there are no problems, he can be finished in eighty minutes then on to Fruithill Court which has twenty seven semi detached bungalows. This takes him a little longer.

He knocks on the first door then opens it with the key and shouts into the bedroom

'Everything alright Mrs Murray?'

'Fine thank you Mr O'Meara!'

That's what he likes to hear. He tries not to engage in any further conversation. He ticks off her name on his clipboard and moves on. In exactly two hours and forty three minutes he is finished. It is important that he notifies the office immediately if there are any irregularities……. People are waiting.

Today there are no irregularities. It is another clean sheet for the Dead Counter – the third one this week. He smiles. The people will have to wait a little longer!

The Dark Hedges

Christopher Moore

A private little kingdom, cut off from the world. You can see why they use this place as a setting for the fantastical. The autumn sun filters through the trees and casts a golden aura around the entire stretch of road, making the wood crimson, the leaves saffron, the grass emerald, and the very air shimmering with a magical hue. In those few moments as the focus of the light shifts, you think you can make out tiny shapes, little dancing lights, darting in and out of your vision, concealing themselves just a fraction of a second too late. You think you can detect a sweet fragrance on the wind, sifting its way through the branches at irregular intervals, as though trying to let something of the outside world in. And you believe, the longer you pause there, the longer you stop to listen, really listen, that you can hear voices. Faint, youthful, restless voices, echoing through the leaves. A strange children's choir, whispering secrets from tops of trees and depths of earth. Suggesting a meeting place, a halfway point, a gathering of souls, some patient, some frustrated, all waiting to journey on to somewhere new.

But, not all the voices are innocent. Or childlike. You can feel that the place is under a spell, an enchantment. Bestowed with a sense of tranquillity, yes, of peace, of escape from the world at large, but... The longer you stay, the longer you allow yourself to bask in that peace... What, then? Because there are definitely other voices besides the mischievous chatter of hidden children and restless travellers. Voices far less playful. There is something watching you. Not restless, but focused. Concentrated. Interested only in you. Observing everything you do, every move you make. You think you can hear it laughing softly to itself the longer you linger and the more the world outside the trees begins to fade from your memory. Laughter at once as soft as the autumn breeze around you, yet laced with a sharper quality that suddenly makes the crimson of the trees around you take on a more unsettling hue. You notice that colour, that crimson, with fresh eyes, its vibrancy, its dark purity, and with a trickle of sweat down your brow, you wonder for the first time just where exactly you are. You wonder what is watching you, waiting. Waiting for the laughing children to fade away until only you are left, isolated and exposed. You realise suddenly that you have lingered too long. You are in a slow, calculated trap.

And yet…

Don't you hear another voice? Hovering on the fringes of the leaves, barely a whisper, but a familiar one. Very familiar. Growing in urgency and insisting that you listen. Listen very carefully.

The whisper grows steadily into a call, into a cry, an insistent pleading from outside the trees, that this is a false refuge. Begging you to listen. Begging you to turn back. And you want to. You want to listen to the call, want to run towards it, away from this place and the other voice that wants you to stay. But you're no longer sure if you can.

You decide. You take a deep breath, and place one heavy foot in front of the other. Willing the enchantment to break. And you hope for the best.

Spectrum

Cathy Carson

It is the Saturday before Christmas and I swear every damn soul in Cornmarket seems intent on walking through me. My ears are bitten, bone marrow cold and the rain has seeped through so that I feel I am being washed away.

Leo holds my hand like he did as a toddler. His frame is now 6ft 2in, his weight 16st and his gait only slightly better.

He walks with his head down to avoid eye contact, using the rhythm of my steps as a guide.

A black Labrador ambles toward us panting, his tongue lolling to the side and I feel Leo stiffen and stop.

'It's ok,' I whisper in a tone that I know calms him. Soft, slow, low and not like me at all really. But I know it works, and today I am going with what works.

' Coffee!' he shouts, loud enough that people stare, and I realise that he hadn't noticed the flipping dog at all.

'Coffee!' Louder this time, letting go of my hand to flap his long arms and stamp his feet.

'No coffee, we need to get home Leo. No coffee and no nonsense.'

I am exhausted, patience paper thin, but he is anchored to the ground, ignoring me and I feel my face colour and my temper swell. I hold out a hand, which he bats away before taking two bold steps toward the coffee shop.

I need to choose my battles.

'Don't you dare,' I mutter. 'Don't you dare have a meltdown in the middle of Cornmarket. Not today son, please.'

The hairs are raised on the back of my neck and the pain in my chest reminds me to breathe.

Teenagers have gathered in the background, mobile phones at the ready. A flush creeps from my chest to my cheeks.

When he was younger the meltdowns would terrify me. He would throw himself to the ground, limbs flailing, foaming at the mouth like a rabid beast, while I froze with horror, not knowing how to make it stop.

Afterwards, I would sit on the floor with his head in my lap and stroke his hair, as much to soothe myself as him. I had no idea how to love this child. I was empty, hollow, as if someone had carved out my very core.

It was years before I realised I was grieving – for the healthy child I thought I had a right to, for the husband that couldn't cope, for all I used to be and who I would never become.

I remember the exact moment it changed. We were on holiday in Portrush, staying in a dilapidated two berth caravan. Leo was five. It had rained all week and I was desperate to get him outside. We donned raincoats and wellingtons and headed to the rock pools, buckets and nets in hand.

The sun struggled through dark clouds casting spotlights on the patches of still water in the rock pools.

Leo hunkered down, reaching out carefully to touch the water with his finger. He giggled as the ripples made their way to the edge, and eyes wide with wonder, he looked straight at me.

Not past me or through me.

Straight at me, his eyes locked on mine.

I saw for the first time the way the sun sprinkled gold on his eyelashes. The way laughter punctured his cheeks with dimples. He clapped his hands, fingers splayed and I crouched cautiously beside him.

'Circles,' he boasted as though he had invented them, his laughter making its way like birdsong through the air.

'Yes Leo, you clever boy, those are circles,' I was shouting, lost in the moment. But then he was gone again as quickly as he had arrived, silent once more, face flat, picking the moss from the stone.

But it didn't matter.

Something had connected, we had connected.

My boy was reachable and I was determined to make it happen again.

In Cornmarket, the streetlights turn raindrops to fireflies above our heads. I watch him closer now, looking for the tell-tale signs that this is something other than defiance.

He isn't tapping on his thigh or rocking on his heels, and there is no low hum that often comes before an episode. There is nothing. But he is growing roots in the ground.

He is huffing.

'Come on Leo'

I try. But immediately I know that the tone is off, too harsh, and I watch his face crumple into well-worn creases as hot fat tears sear his face.

The aroma from the coffee shop smells so good, and I am beginning to think it was an ingenious idea. Standing my ground isn't worth this. Nothing is worth this. The guilt is so heavy I have trouble stepping towards him with my outstretched hand.

'Come on then big lad, let's grab that coffee.'

There it is. That smile, the punctured dimples in his cheeks as he looks straight at me.

My forever boy takes my hand.

Solitude

Christopher Moore

Yap. Yap. Yap. Yap. Yap.

Was this it? Was this her life, was this the end point she had worked towards for fifty years? Scrimped and saved and sacrificed for one ungrateful child after another, endured a worse-than-useless husband, an unfulfilling career, putting the needs of others before her own, year after year with no reward, all for...this? To sit in a dreary front room with stained blinds and dusty cushions, faded carpet, and drab wallpaper? Central heating struggling to warm the house, ancient television in the corner forever on the blink, and, best of all, a parade of misbehaved little shits pelting stones at her window from the garden? Was this what she had worked towards? Was this her life's reward for years of putting her own desires aside?

Yap. Yap. Yap. Yap. Yap.

The dog would not shut up. No matter how much she shouted, or hissed, or spat, or ultimately tried to ignore. No matter how long she sat there, determining not to get up and humour the beast after only just feeding it. Still, it yelped on, bark after bark, demanding to be heard. To have its perceived needs seen to. To have her tend to it.

Yap. Yap. Yap. Yap. Yap.

Attend me, it seemed to shout. *Give me what I want.*

Yap. Yap. Yap. Yap. Yap.

No more. Something in her snapped, broke apart. A lifetime of repressed frustration, escaping in one violent burst. Fury and resentment and disappointment spilled out of her in a wave, and she leapt from her seat, dust flying from the fabric as she rose, and launched herself across the room, straight for it, hurtling so fast the beast didn't have time to react. She reached for the creature's neck. Wrapped her hands tightly around it. And squeezed.

The body would never be discovered.

She made sure there wasn't very much of anything left to find, and that was that. Afterwards, she went outside to the back garden, with a glass and the bottle of wine her eldest had passed off as a present on Christmas Day, retrieved a plastic chair caked in grime and neglect from the shed, and sat down amongst the shin-high blades of grass and miniature forest of dandelions, her feet quickly disappearing into the growth.

She never sat out here. Ever. Always felt too self-conscious, too paranoid, somehow, that there would be eyes on her within moments, that the neighbours would be watching from their upstairs windows, that the little bastards at the front would somehow get wind of it, and hurry round to peer over the back fence and marvel at the old biddy from Number 3 sitting drinking alone in the middle of the day.

Well, let them. Let Imelda from Number 5 spy on her all she liked. Let her judge, let her assume, let her silently disapprove. To hell with her. To hell with them all. It was her property. She had no job to be at, and if the government expected her to survive on the pittance she collected from the post office every week, she could at least do what she bloody well liked with her time.

She wondered as she looked around when the grass had last been touched. When it had last felt the slice of a blade cutting through it. She couldn't remember. Perhaps Gerald had given it a turn a couple of years ago out of a momentary sense of obligation, but certainly no more recently than that. It really was pathetic, now that she looked at it. Now that she took in just how unkempt her little patch of earth was. A testament, a monument to how little she was cared about by anyone. How uninterested her children were. Brought up to show discipline and respect, only to largely walk out of her life as though she were some sort of hated former employer, rather than the woman who had gone through hours of labour for them. It was galling, the more she thought about it. So, she didn't. Instead, she poured herself a glass, set the bottle down into the undergrowth, gave a silent toast to the memory of the dog before it had become insufferable, and, sitting back in the chair, closed her eyes in the afternoon sun.

Rain

Jay Faulkner

The rain continued to fall; I didn't think it would ever stop and wondered if this was how the World ended. I'd never been a religious man - the last time I'd even stepped foot inside Church was when my mother was buried – but, right then, I was ready to fall on my knees and beg for God's help because, for the life of me, I couldn't think of anything left to try. When He didn't answer all I was left with were questions.

Why couldn't the rain have waited a little longer? It hadn't rained for days so why now? Why couldn't the boys have played elsewhere? Anywhere?

Nearly a month's worth of rain had fallen in less than a day, flooding most of the low lying area of Witney; enough rain to trap two boys in the culvert that, right now, looked more like a white-water rafting area than a landlocked pipe.

I couldn't stop the shivering that overtook my body; tried to pretend it was just the fact that I'd been up to my neck in frigid water for nearly fourteen minutes that caused it. My mother, God rest her, would have said someone had walked over my grave. I didn't believe in that superstitious nonsense. To be safe I crossed myself anyway. I'd worked for fire and rescue for nearly twenty years but could never remember feeling so cold. Another shiver cut short as a shout of triumph broke out amongst the men – my colleagues, my friends – and a coughing boy was pulled out of the pipe and hauled back towards me. I felt the small form pass through my hands as I lifted him to the waiting ambulance crew.

He was so young.

My own boy, Steven, was older and yet I still thought of him as my baby. And there was someone else's child – someone else's baby – still trapped in the flooded pipe.

Please God, bring him out. Please.

Water coursed down their bodies as the men went back to work. Even from here, in the dimly lit Autumn evening, I could see the blue tinge on their lips. I was chilled deep in my own bones and knew – God, how I wished that I didn't – that hope was fading fast. We couldn't last much longer in the freezing cold of the rising water so, without our gear, without our training, what hope did he have?

How long had it been, now? How long had he been trapped by the metal grate?

Looking down at my watch I had to wipe the streaming water away from my eyes to see that it had been nearly twenty minutes.

Twenty minutes in the cold.

Submerged.

In the dark.

Alone.

Then, finally, I watched as - without a sound - hands gently carried another boy out of the water; skin pale; body limp.

Unmoving.

I closed my eyes, thankful for the rain that hid my tears.

Keady Graveyard Sunday

Damien Mallon

You always met me near the angel
Down by the concrete path.
We'd replay all the matches
And have a real good laugh.
There'd be talk about dogs
And where the pheasants lie.
Then we'd cup our hands in prayer
And try hard not to smile.
When they read the list of the departed
You always looked at me.
As we heard the names of those we knew
And stood there solemnly.
I hope you're near the angel
For you're not here this year.
But still my eyes went round the crowd
For the one that I'd held dear.
And only then I missed you
And I hurt for your 'bit of crack'
But only when they read your name
I knew you'd not be back.

Previously Published in *Reading the Trees* by Damien Mallon

Lonely Hearts

Kieran Mc Gurk

The last thing I wanted to do was clear out my father's suits. This was a man with no secrets and the brown and oatmeal row in his wardrobe was a concertina of dull, drab shadows. My mother never commented on his clothes when he was alive and now, a year after his funeral, she still wouldn't.

I could hear her in the next room, an occasional clearing of the throat, 'Ha hahhamem,' very much like he used to

She wouldn't come in until the job was finished. Some of the better stuff could go to Oxfam but most of it would be taken from here to a place of execution. Suffocation by black bag of stuff already gassed by mothballs.

I kept the jackets until last. Twelve of them. One of them would betray him. A navy blazer. Gold buttons. Curious. Never worn. It coughed up a neatly folded square of Basildon Bond, matching blue envelope, stamp et al. In his finest copperplate writing,

'Londonderry Debonair. Widower. WLTM lady, 50 to 60 N/S, for dance, romance and more.'

Gawd, he even knew the lingo.

It was dated around the time when mum had her bypass. Poor bugger hoped she would go first. So did the rest of us

Mahogany

Peter Hollywood

His father was in a knife fight once, during the Second World War, with an on-leave American GI. It happened in the busy market town his father, and later he, grew up in, located close to the border.

His father owned a public house on the main street a few doors down from The Frontier Cinema. American troops would have been stationed in camp-sites scattered around the countryside and, at weekends, the soldiers would flood into the town on leave. However, the knife-fight took place early one week-day. His father had just opened the doors with Slim McAteer the sole client requiring admission at such an early hour; he quickly ensconced himself out of the way, in the snug at the main street side of the bar – there was an entrance in off the side street as well – and subsequently missed the whole action, oblivious to the two large men crashing into furniture, counter and walls. The snug, it should be said, was meant really for female clientele where they could sup in peace, ordering sherry and gin through the confessional of the hatch door that opened onto the counter at that end. Slim McAteer favoured the snug at that early hour.

At that time, his father washed the empties and bottled, capped and labelled the beer himself. Arthur Guinness supplied him with customised labels for the bottles. Having let Slim McAteer in and served him his customary bottle of stout and measure of rum, his father had disappeared out the back to retrieve a newly bottled crate of beer from the bottling store.

The way back in led past the stairway winding up to the living quarters. Glancing up, he suddenly stopped in his tracks at the sight of the uniformed American half-way up the stairs. At this point, his teenaged younger sister, just in from morning mass, must also have seen the GI for she let out a scream from above. The soldier had obviously followed her home and in through the side door, stalking her on up the stairs.

His father let the crate drop, took the stairs two at a time, yanked the soldier by the shoulder and pitched him down the stairs into the back hall, swimming now with beer. The soldier was quickly to his feet, though he had trouble steadying himself what with slipping in the spillage and then barking his shin on the discarded, wooden beer-crate. In such stumbling fashion, he disappeared into the bar area. Thomas's father leapt down after him.

Turning the corner, he found himself confronted with the GI, seething, crouched over with a flick knife open in his right hand. He immediately regretted not lifting a bottle from the crate for protection; he even fleetingly thought of fashioning a vambrace from his long, white, vintner's apron.

-His arm, Thomas's father would say. I quickly realised that I had to get a grip of his right arm and just hold on for dear life.

Possibly still dazed from the tumble over the crate of beer, the soldier did not anticipate his assailant's swift move. His father got a vice-like grip of the right arm and, linked like this, the two men waltzed on into the bar cursing and struggling and strangling and whirling each other around.

What saved his father was the ancient and imposing structure of the dark brown mahogany counter that ran the length of the public bar. At one point, the two combatants came careening off the back wall and they collided with the counter. The tip of the blade of the flick-knife struck the unyielding, obsidian surface of the wood and bounced right back off it. The soldier must not have had a firm grasp of the handle for, at the shock of impact, the blade slid up his grip, slicing open the palm of his hand, incising on up over his wrist. The knife clattered to the flag-stone floor and, extricating himself, the GI exited the bar, baying, his father always said, like some wounded beast.

As he went, spraying blood all over the place, Slim McAteer chose that moment to slide open the hatch and, spying Thomas's father standing panting where he was, promptly requested another rum and stout.

-If it's not too much bother, he added.

-The knife, Dad, Thomas's older brother had once asked. What did you do with the knife?

They were both hoping that it existed as some sort of grisly, family heirloom.

-I gave it to Joseph Slow Waters; as evidence.

Joseph Slow Waters was a military policeman with whom their father had become friendly. He was of the Navaho nation and was enraged when his father reported the incident. He took the knife away, vowing to be on the look-out for a GI with a heavily bandaged hand and wrist.

Thomas's father never discovered if the culprit was caught. Almost overnight, the camps emptied and the soldiers disappeared; they found themselves on board a fleet of warships, forging their way across a porter-dark sea, bound for the beaches of Normandy.

A soldier with a heavily bandaged hand and wrist would quickly find familiars there.

There were soldiers too, in the town, when Thomas was growing up. These ones, as you know, were not on leave

Mansfield House

Pamela Mary Brown

Brigadier George Wilson raised a confident hand to speak.

'Of course, it reminds me of meeting Mr Churchill.' His face altered and became downcast as he grabbed his chin in confused recollection. 'It was either Plymouth or Southampton?'

'Yes, Brigadier Wilson. We know you met Mr Churchill. It's time for bingo. Take your seat. Come on Georgie Porgie.' Frank gripped George's upper arm and led him quick time across the floor of the common room. He shoved George onto a seat among the other elderly residents.

The room had been a ballroom before Mansfield House was converted into a care home. It still had the marble fireplace and high windows facing onto the three-tiered garden. The wallpaper showed a tracery of vines with sparrows and starlings. The furniture was practical as many of the faux leather chairs had restrainers to prevent people falling. The sliding sash windows had net-curtains. The pictures suspended from the picture rail were a series of landscapes and cityscapes. The bookcase with paperbacks, CDs and DVDs was topped with a TV screen always on like the ceiling lights.

Nurse Rodgers issued the bingo books and pens. With her usual smile to the residents, she made a flirtatious glance at Frank who had sat at a table with the *Super Select Electronic Bingo* machine. She snapped each bingo book securely onto a blue clipboard and got everyone's attention with rebukes and reprimands.

'There you go, Josephine. You had a bit of good luck last week. Pauline, stop giggling and take your book. Anne, remember to clean your mouth after dinner. Use the hanky tucked up your sleeve. Don't spit on it. Wilfred! Keep your hands to yourself. Oh dear, Brigadier George.' Nurse Rodgers placed the final clipboard on his lap; not impressed with the military man or his former rank.

A door opened. George blinked walking into the garden. His steps somnambulatory as he mounted the wheelchair ramp leading to a fountain. The ground was wet. His slippers were soon soaking. The lawn was the length of a bowling green. The laurel hedging swelled in growth that required pruning. Rhododendrons gone wild were for termination. Insect life in summer and late autumn threatened everyone outdoors. George arrived at the fountain feeling frail and fatigued. A flowering weed lured him to sniff it. Margaret liked flowers. Who was Margaret? If he touched this flower maybe he would remember Margaret.

'George! BRIGADIER!' A male voice bellowed.

George pulled at the flower.

'George!' The male voice again.

Suddenly, a pain in his arm.

'I took a hit. Retreat to the ridge. Hold back. Defend the house.' George cried out and stumbled forward.

'He bloody thinks he's at war,' Frank laughed. 'Brigadier. Enemy snipers. Retreat in single file!' Frank said mockingly as George tried to resist his grip.

'Georgie.' Nurse Rodgers shouted. 'Frank needs to get you inside.'

Frank pulled George harder and he fell onto the wet grass.

'I'm not going to make it,' his face was frightened as he appealed for their help to lift him. They did but roughly.

'My father's face is bruised!' George Junior was distraught at Nurse Rodgers who held a bundle of medical reports.

'Your father fell out of bed. Again.' She replied. 'Isn't that right Brigadier?'

The bed rails were raised, and George stared at the ceiling.

'My father's in bed in the middle of the afternoon!'

'He's been asleep on and off all day, and refused to attend our gala bingo,' Nurse Rodgers's voice was harsh.

'You can't lock him up like this.'

'And he fell during a walk outdoors after lunch,' she said stolidly as Frank entered the room.

'Surely there is supervision?' George Junior turned to Frank who leaned by the door.

'It's for his own safety, he's a handful,' Frank grunted.

'Mr Wilson. I understand your distress, but Mansfield House has the highest standards. Your father is a particular high risk. His dementia is not only a danger to himself but other residents.' Nurse Rodgers added.

'Pigs,' muttered the Brigadier.

'What's that Dad?'

'Mr Churchill shook my hand.'

'That's right Dad,' George Junior took his father's hand.

'Did I tell you what he said?' Brigadier George's eyes were wide.

'I know what Churchill said, Dad. You told me. About the pigs, and the cats and dogs. Churchill told you that 'Dogs look up to us. Cats look down on us. Pigs treat us as equals."

'No,' Brigadier George cried out. 'Pigs treat you like pigs.'

Mother, Son & Ghost

Malachi Kelly

At 6.15am I was rocked awake, by a worn-out mother of 8 children, to rise and get ready for the mile walk to St Patricks Cathedral and serve mass. It was winter in the 1960s

Serving mass on one of the Cathedral's altars at any time was looked on as Holy Privilege and when asked, was taken as a blessing on the family. I wasn't asked. I was told.

I wolfed a quick bowl of porridge as mother dressed me in knitted woolly hat, duffle coat and short trousers.

The sturdy brown paper bag holding my Gutties and surplice was stuck under my oxter and a promise of a good spanking, if I dropped them, rang in my ears. Our back door opened and winter's cold arm slipped around my shoulders and pulled me into its blackness as Mummy slammed the door on me.

Now when you wore short trousers your thighs are exposed to what meteorologists called 'east wind.' This wind travels all the way from satanic Communist Russia 'to hack and redden those delicate parts of Irish Catholic boys legs and try to prevent them doing the Lord's service.'So I was told. I was a soldier 'fighting against the commies and the colder the east wind the holier I was.'

The truth is my mother couldn't afford new trousers for me; I had to wait 'till I was big enough for a brother's hand-me-downs

I hated Russia!

My daily commi-no began by me pulling up my socks and pulling down my short trousers as I walked out our gate and estate to the main road. A battery torch, my sole protection to the dark, its beam barely visible.

Approaching the main road the first street light illuminated the junction while moths danced and fluttered around its meagre heat. No one else was about. I was a lone soldier. The Lone Ranger heading off on Trigger to sort out the Commie Indians. Slapping my backside with the brown bag I bolted into the dark.

At the local shop, I turned right taking a short cut, in my mind heading the Injins off at the pass!

Crossing another main road I went through the Cathedral turnstile and on to the path leading up to the rear of the church and its scarcity. This was ambush country!

Once again in complete darkness, my only light being the useless torch.

It's only in more recent years that the Cathedral has been spotlit for the faithful to 'see the light' but right now it was blind faith that guided me.

As I ran along the narrow tarmac footpath, to a break in the hedge which dissects this backfield, I saw it.

A ghostly white shape appeared on the other side.

It stopped, and seemed to be shivering, just as I was.

Neither of us moved. I couldn't and the ghost wouldn't. One large black eye glared at me defiantly from this shimmering whiteness.

I legged it!

Slapping my thighs as hard as I could with my paper bag I was back on the main road emptying my 6 gun torch behind me. Shock propelled me up Banbrook to the Shambles and the front gates of the Cathedral. Its clock face told me time was not on my side as I flew up the granite steps.

A greater fear now consuming me that of being late for the priest, and, would he tell my Mother?

I should have shot the ghost in the eye when I had the chance.

Reaching the sacristy in a lather of sweat I pushed open the enormous oak doors to.

'You're late, young man.' It was the Sacristan. 'Lucky for you there's been a death during the night. Father's not here yet. You look as if you've seen a ghost and look at the state of your surplus!'

'In nomonie Patris et spiritus sancti.'

'Et cum spiritu tuo,' I replied in my best Latin and quietly thanked God for taking one of his faithful 'home' last night.

Fifteen minutes later, with mass over and the morning now clear and bright I braved the back path.

Whoever heard of ghosts during the day? Anyway, I had reloaded my pistol torch, just to be sure.

Slowing as I neared the gap, gun ready and eyes peeled, my trail was suddenly blocked again by a large, mainly white, Friesian cow.

This cowboy had been spooked by a real cow!

My Doll's Funeral

Doreen Mc Bride

I was five years of age when there was a funeral in Manna Grove.

It was great!

Our eyes stood out on stalks as we watched. Weeping women in sombre black, with a large, flower-covered box being carried out of the house. A huge black hearse crawled along the middle of the road followed by four men carrying the coffin and what seemed like hundreds of dark-suited men, carrying proper hats, not just everyday dunchers. It was a solemn procession with large black limousines moving towards Orangefield Presbyterian Church.

Our street rarely saw a car never mind a limousine! Cars were a rare event in the late forties.

We were so impressed we decided to play funerals.

First of all, we had to find a suitable grave. We decided on the rough piece of ground in my back garden. It was meant to be a vegetable patch but grew nothing but weeds, snails and slugs. It would be a great place to bury a body and nobody would ever know.

Jane rushed home and came back proudly carrying a shoebox. I got a spade and we took turns digging.

Trouble arose because we hadn't a body to bury.

I felt I had done my bit providing a grave.

Jane and Freda thought as we couldn't bury a human, it would have to be a doll, and it should be my doll as I was in the best position to look after it. After all, the grave was in my garden.

I thought I don't like Jennifer. I wouldn't miss her so I said, 'My doll, Jennifer's no good. Let's bury her.'

Freda got a roll of black crepe paper. We cut it into three equal bits, folded each bit in two, cut a hole cut in the middle, stuck our heads through the holes and stood back admiring each other.

Jane said we needed hats so we borrowed black hats from our mothers. Needless to say, our mothers didn't know their good hats had been borrowed!

Jennifer had a lovely funeral. We folded her long cloth legs up around her ears, tucked her into the shoebox, carried it around the square on our shoulders before placing it reverently in the hole.

Freda said a long boring prayer, we threw buttercups and daisies on top of the 'coffin' before covering it with earth and flowers. We all had a good 'cry' while Jane recited,

'Ashes to ashes, dust to dust,

If the booze don't get you, the weemen must.'

She'd heard her Daddy saying that one night when he'd come home drunk after attending Aunty Bessie's funeral and thought it was what people said in graveyards. It seemed appropriate.

During the night I dreamt poor Jennifer was crying. She couldn't move. She wanted her Mummy.

I was filled with remorse. How could I have buried her alive?

I sneaked out of bed, faced the terrors of the night, found the grave, dug her up, dusted her down, kissed her better and took her to bed. No more funerals for Jennifer! From that moment on she was my favourite doll.

Only a Clockwork Heart

by Kerry Buchanan

Bianca danced with steps light and true, the envy of all – until the moment when her clockwork heart began to fail: *ba boom, ba... ba... ba boom.*

Clutching her chest, she stumbled, then fell to her knees on the cold stone floor. She tilted her face up and raised her arms, beseeching.

Prince Gorgeous stepped away from her, disdain written plain in the curl of his upper lip. 'You are flawed, not perfect as I was led to believe.' Then he spun on his raised heels and abandoned her in the middle of the dancefloor. The other dancers parted to let him through.

Bianca's flailing hand touched and gripped the edge of a kettledrum. The drummer had blue eyes and a symmetrical face, mouth set in a half-smile that could never change. One of her own kind: an automaton, created purely for the pleasure of humans.

'Help me?' she pleaded.

He brought the first stick down onto the skin. *Boom.* An answering reflex kicked off in her chest.

The orchestra wavered, distracted by the unexpected beat, but they recovered so quickly that the dancers barely noticed. Then it came again.

Boom.

Bianca's clockwork heart answered the call – *ba boom.* Her cheeks flushed from porcelain-white to the faintest of rose-pinks.

Boom boom ba boom boom ba boom boom....

One by one, the orchestra tumbled through disharmony into silence, until the kettledrum played on alone.

Bianca rose to her feet and stepped out onto the floor, blue silks swaying, head held high. Light as thistledown, she swirled.

'Who is she?' the other dancers whispered. 'She's beautiful! So graceful.'

On the grand staircase, Prince Gorgeous looked back, and his breath caught in his throat.

The drummer didn't seem to notice as the conductor approached with a face like fury – until the sticks were snatched from his hands.

As the kettledrum fell silent, Bianca stumbled to a halt.

Then a snare drum picked up the beat, followed by the bass drum.

A vein throbbed in the conductor's neck. He dropped the sticks and set off towards the snare drummer, but before he'd taken two steps, one of the cellists began to pluck out a new melody. A heartbeat later, the harp took up a rippling harmony and after a short period of tuneless confusion, the entire woodwind section joined in.

The conductor was incandescent in his rage. Behind him, the first timpanist picked up his sticks from the floor and returned to his kettledrum.

Prince Gorgeous couldn't take his eyes from Bianca as she swayed to the new rhythm. The kettle-drummer raised the tempo, and her steps matched his beat until she soared into the air in a leap, caught by one of the other dancers and passed on to the next, hand-to-hand, feet flying across the marble floor.

One by one, ladies and gentlemen began to follow her lead until gradually the entire ballroom took up the new form. It was free and full of joyful expression, very different from the stifled rigidity of their country's traditional dance.

The prince clenched his fists, aching for what might have been. He'd had her in his arms; held her close. Bianca had almost belonged to him, but now, it seemed, the hearts of his people belonged to her.

La Grande Odalisque

P.V. Wolseley

The score seemed simple: Paint a pendant piece; east to my sister's west – back to her front. And the sketches – true to life – seemed to make a simple job of it. But when the artist came to the canvas, he picked up a new tune.

'See only the sublime,' he said, closing his eyes as if listening to music faint or far.

'Sublime,' he said, eyes still closed, nodding.

'Line,' he said, as if he had recognised the melody. And then he smiled, as if giving himself up to it.

He let the line lead him, tracing it long, slow, sinuous like smoke from a hookah. All fell into place easily, coming together as if according to sheet music written in air. I became a strange melody; all wrong – and right: a dislocated hip that wouldn't work any other way; an arm too long and long enough; a neck twisted, just so. The rest is colour harmonies and counterpoint: the caress of silk on skin, the felted give of velvet, the sigh of feathers falling limp in the evening heat. The climax builds along my back – but so slowly, that he himself took a step back, to check the score. He returned, sure as a calligrapher, and cast the line in a slow-motion swoop that dropped but never fell, like a note left quivering almost – but not quite – too long. And there he left it. And here I am: revealing as much as a woman possibly can with her back turned.

Hurricane Glamping

Elaine Toal

I had painted the scene for them, miles and miles of deserted beach, the rolling hills of Donegal tumbling down to the coastline. 'Let's take the girls to Dunfanaghy,' I said to my husband. 'They will love it!'

Too old, or too soft, for camping, we decided to go 'glamping'. A few clicks on a shiny screen and the whole thing was booked.

The girls packed a bag each with all the essentials that a five year old and a two year old might need on holiday. A naked doll with a missing arm, a teddy bear with a ripped ear, and the beloved Moo, without whom no holiday is complete.

With the car loaded we set off on our adventure. Under the chatter of the children and the hum of the engine on the road, I heard the weather forecaster mention something about storm force winds, a remnant from hurricane Gertrude set to hit the coastline this weekend. My husband saw the shadow of doubt crossing my face. 'Stop worrying, it'll be fine.' He reassured me.

Three hours and two confined children later, we spilled out of the car and into the campsite taking a first look at our home for the weekend. It was a canvas bell tent. It looked pretty robust but with the words 'storm force' echoing in my ears I still felt a little anxious. 'Maybe we should check if there is a B&B available' I floated the idea half-heartedly knowing that at this point, on an August bank holiday weekend we had no chance.

Unzipping the canvas door, the girls exploded into the tent. 'There are beds!' They exclaimed, jumping from one to another. A chorus of 'this one is mine' rang out as they marked their territories. Their enthusiasm carried me along and into the tent I went.

Glamping had conjured up images of sipping champagne while wearing wellies or luxury paired with a little bit of the great outdoors.

The only thing luxurious about this so far was the price. I sat on the bed as the girls ran around in excited circles.

'There's no heat,' I whispered to my husband, 'the bed is damp.' He gave me his best 'we are here now, let's make the most of it' look and led us all off to Marble Hill beach.

Between showers of rain that came from nowhere, horizontal and unforgiving, the girls revelled in building sandcastles. Zipped up to the neck in fleece lined coats, wellies on and hats pulled down low, they made the most of a summer holiday in Donegal. They ran to the water, splashing in the shallows; the sea a steel grey, reflecting the stormy sky above. A cold, dark, wet August day did not dampen their spirits.

As night fell we settled into our tent. For a while there was calm. I lay there, listening to the sounds beyond the thin layer of canvas that separated us from the night sky. I could hear the hushed tones of other families settling in for the night and the excited chatter of young people setting out for a night on the town, whispering loudly as their footsteps faded into the darkness.

I suppose I must have slept at some point, but when Hurricane Gertrude made landfall, we knew about it. The soft rustle in the trees became louder and stronger, and I imagined the branches swaying and bending under the strain of the storm. In the dim light I watched the canvas roof rise and fall with the movement of the wind. Then the rain came, relentless and unabated. Every drop that hit the tent seemed louder and stronger than the last. And I knew, with certainty it would wake the children.

At home, on a normal night, you can hear her footsteps as she creeps softly into our room. A whisper in my ear about a bad dream and she settles to sleep beside me. But in the tent she catapulted herself from her bed to mine, wide eyed in terror!

'The rain! It's so loud! Is it going to come in?' her panicked voice causing her sister to open her eyes. The four of us huddled together under the damp duvet and listened to the storm beyond the canvas. The howling wind and hammering rain gave them a fitful night's sleep. But like all stormy nights, it passes with the dawn. Pale faced and shivering, they awoke and declared their love of glamping, demanding a cup of tea to warm them up and another trip to Marble Hill beach. And that's exactly what we did.

Hurricane Glamping was first published in *Circling Round Conformity*, published in 2018 by Dunfanaghy Writers' Circle and edited by Alf McCreary.

Scáile Dheirdre

Máire Dinny Wren

Thóg Deirdre moll billí ón urlár. Dhruid sí suas an bocsa litreach ionas nach dtiocfadh leo níos mó billí a chur isteach fríd an doras. Lá arna mhárach cuireadh na billí isteach an fhuinneog a bhí leathfhoscailte le haer an tsamhraidh a ligint isteach. Chuir Deirdre na billí sa chuisneoir áit a raibh billí eile stóráilte aici. Bhordáil sí na fuinneoga le clárthaí, ionas nach dtiocfadh leo tuilleadh billí a chur isteach fríothu.

An lá dár gcionn, tháinig báillí agus stróc siad leo na ballaí agus an díon agus na troscáin agus cha raibh dadaidh fágtha ach na billí. Rinne Deirdre leaba as na billí agus luigh sí orthu an oíche sin. Lá arna mhárach tháinig an fhearthainn. D'éalaigh Deirdre go dtí an choillidh agus chuir sí fúithi ansin. Mhair sí ar luibheanna, ar chnónna agus ar bhláthanna. Bhí sí ar a sáimhín só.

Lá amháin ghearr sábhadóirí na crainn uilig. D'éalaigh Deirdre isteach i ngleann domhain agus chuir sí fúithi ansin. Mhair sí ar bhric, ar luibheanna is ar na glasraí a d'fhás ar fud an ghleanna. Bhí sí sona sásta.

Lá amháin tháinig bodach agus d'fhógair gur leisean an gleann agus go raibh sé le caisleán a thógáil ann. Díbríodh Deirdre. Bhain sí an sliabh amach. Mhair sí ar chaora agus ar fhíoruisce tobair. Bhí sí sona sáthach.

Lá amháin tháinig boc mór agus d'fhógair gur leisean an cnoc, go raibh sé le feirm ghaoithe a thógáil ann agus dhíbir sé Deirdre. Chonaic Deirdre eastát tréigthe ar imeall an tsráidbhaile. Chuir sí fúithi ann. Cha raibh sí ábalta bia a sheiftiú mar go raibh an talamh clúdaithe le tarra agus stroighin. Mhair sí ar na ceannóga agus ar phiocarsach a d'fhág na forbróirí ina ndiaidh. Bhí sí sásta, cé go raibh sí beo ar éigean.

Nuair a thoisigh siad a leagaint an eastáit thréigthe go talamh, níor chronaigh siad Deirdre agus ní fhaca aonduine a scáile ag siúl san eastát san oíche. Nuair a fuair siad a corp, dúradh gur dhuine siúil í agus gur gnáthchúrsaí an tsaoil a thug a bás.

Tá *Scáile Dheirdre* sa chnuasacht gearrscéalta *Go mBeinnse Choíche Saor* le Máire Dinny Wren a d'fhoilsigh Éabhlóid in 2016.

READY

Cathy Carson

'Please come love, your wee Daddy keeps asking for you,
and I think it will be hours now, rather than days.'
Do you know your nurse sounds like a petulant child?
'I don't care,' I spit the words down the phone.
'You make sure to tell him I don't care and that I am not coming.'
But I slam down the phone,
grab my coat and keys.
I am coming to see you.
I am ready.
Are you?

At six years old I was already afraid of you.
In your presence, tiny explosions of fear caused chaos in my
thoughts,
a stutter in my speech and an awkwardness
that delighted your cruelty no end.

I hope you are learning what fear feels like.

At eight years old, I could tell how drunk you were,
by the pace of your footsteps on the path.
How angry, by the sound of your breath.
I would lie stock still and listen through my skin…
wincing at every slap,
every blow,
every toxic word you spewed,
the air peppered with foul language
and my head filled with scenes I did not want to see.

At eleven years, old I knew that my call
was a cup slammed three times on a table.
The scenes were no longer in my head.
I would get up from my bed,
limbs heavy,
head racing.
And I would sit ram rod straight,
all night long sometimes
and wait for the mind games to end
and the slaps and punches to begin.
I would imagine shooting lasers of hate at you
'cartoon villan' style.
In my head
I watched you shrivel
and beg for mercy which
which never came.

And now it seems like my lasers have worked and I can't help it.
I am euphoric with the justice of it.

In your absence we did not speak of it.
The weight of the secret
pushing at the walls of our house
making it impossible to breathe.
My mother,
rocking in the corner.
Long since lost all sense of self
and function.
And so it continued,
your games,
 your rules,
our hell.
I hope you will ask for forgiveness today….it will not be given.

At 15 I slept through my call
and was torn from my bed by my hair
and carried,
legs flailing

down the stairs.
I would not cry.
Within minutes it was over.
No mind games.
There has never been
a sweeter lesson.
I began to push *your* buttons.
I became manipulative,
devisive,
provocative.
Within minutes they would come.
Blow after blessed blow.
The violent sweet shock
momentary respite
from the necrotic
wounds caused by your words.
This was my game now,
these were my rules
and I had learnt from a master.

I hope this cancer is rampaging through you, making your skin creep
and your teeth itch.

At twenty I fought back,
 verbally at first,
 then physically.
Then the night that changed everything.
A mantle clock grabbed in my defence,
a poker grabbed in yours...
which lanced my side,
an inky leaking puddle
that calmed me,
but made you flee.

Later, in the hospital ..... I told
I told a nurse,
a doctor,
a social worker,

the police.
The words delicious and victorious on my tongue.
The following year was a blur…
I remember a refuge…….
a court case,
a protection order,
an exclusion order,
a fine.
Justice,
triumph,
safety.

It has been six years,
I am ready!
Today I will tell you
You had no business
having children you would not love.
That you had no right.
That your stupid little bitch
 now has two first class degrees.
That even though every relationship
where someone *didn't* abuse her
felt like a white knuckle ride,
she held on.
She learned to give love and to receive love,
to love herself.
That she has learned
to stand in the truth of her past
without shame.
That all she has achieved,
all that she is ….
is in spite of you
and not because…….

I am here.
But I cannot see you.
I am pacing now.
Where are you?

How dare you hide from me....
you will not take this moment from me.
I am ready!
And then I hear it....a cup slammed three times against a table.
I spin toward the sound.
And there you are.
Pityful.
Childlike in stature.
An octopus of tubes and wires and leads.
And I cannot move.
Something swells and bursts within my chest.
All my words are lost.
And all the air has left me.
I look into blue eyes that mirror my own.
I watch them glaze
as your head
slumps heavily to the side.
And in this moment....
there are things that I know to be true
with incomprehensible clarity....
That I have nothing but compassion for you.
That I forgive you.
That you are already gone.
And that I......am not ready.

Scoring in the Seventies

Malachi Kelly

What would you think of a Brother-in-law who offered you his two-piece suit?

Not one worn once or twice a year since being purchased on the 'never never' out of Lennox's or John Patrick's.

No, this was a working suit which he plied his trade in night after night, up and down the length of Ireland and beyond.

A country and western' band suit which was seen on the stages of smoke filled hotels and community halls by thousands of sweaty, drunken, screaming teenagers.

'Only 6 more like it in the rest of Ireland,' he said.

'Friggin great,' said I.

The stock reply nowadays would be 'cool.' But in the early seventies, in your mid-teens, last suit being your short legged first communion 'outfit', this turquoise two-piece was 'FRIGGIN GREAT!'

'I'll be the only one at the Shambles dressed in a broad lapelled turquoise suit with fashionably flared trousers...Dead on!'

Wait till the girls cop a load of me with my shoulder length hair, parted in the middle, the long pointed collars of my 'silk' shirt and the raised heels of my pointed shoes. Rod Stewart eat your heart out.

Pure jealousy is always portrayed by a slagging.

'Are you wearing that as a bet?'

'Does your Mummy know you are out like that?' and that was just the lads.

Never get above your station, don't look different or, God forbid, confident - before you're drunk!

But you know you're on to something because the more slagging, the more jealous 'they' are, AND only 6 more like this in Ireland!

Hotel Hillgrove, Monaghan, was our escape from all the pressures of teenage life. We thumbed and begged lifts to this mecca of sound at the weekends to see bands just like the Brother-in-law's and dance the night away.

They may have been great bands but they were peripheral to the main business of 'Scoring.'

And this was when the slagging stopped. As the brightest coloured cock always gets the hen!

The next Saturday night, 7 turquoise-suited lads waited at the Shambles for the minibus to Monaghan. There was going to be some feathers ruffled tonight!

Neamhchiontach go dtí go gcruthaítear a mhalairt

Seán Ó Farraigh

Chuir sí in iúl dom nach mbeadh sí in ann bualadh liom toisc gur thit a deartháir síos an staighre agus go raibh uirthi cuairt a thabhairt air san ospidéal. Tháinig taom gruaime orm nuair a chuala mé an scéala as siocair go raibh mé ag dúil go mór lenár gcoinne an lá ar fad. Oíche iontach, mo phus!

"Shíl mé nár réitigh tú go maith le do dheartháir", a dúirt mé go feargach.

Níor thug sí freagra láithreach dom ach sa deireadh chuala mé guth bog "Cad faoi Dé Máirt, ag an ghnátham?"

"Ní shílim go bhfuil sin ag fóirstean dom ach cuirfidh mé scairt ort dé luain", chaith mé síos an guthán go gasta.

Chuir mé scairt ar mo bhean chéile Caitlín go drogallach ina dhiaidh sin le rá go raibh mé ar an bhealach abhaile. Bhí mé ag obair go mall toisc go raibh neart oibre ar siúl ag an ghníomhaireacht eastáit, ní raibh ach dhá sheachtain fágtha sula bhfoilseofaí torthaí na nArdleibhéal. Níorbh fhada go mbeadh mic léinn nua ag teacht go Béal Feirste! Bíodh sin mar atá, d'imigh mé liom ag ceathrú go dtí a sé toisc go raibh mé ag fiuchadh le fearg.

Nuair a shroic mé an carr áfach, bhí aiféala orm faoin chaoi ar labhair mé le Siobhán. Ní raibh sin tuillte aici agus is cinnte nach raibh sí sásta lena ról i mo shaol grá. Mhothaigh mé go raibh orm comaoin a chúiteamh léi.

"Dosaen rósanna a uasail Ó Baoill", a dúirt mé agus mé ag tochailt i mo phocaí do mo sparán.

"An bhfuil tú i bponc le Caitlín arís a Liam?" a dúirt uasal Ó Baoill go spraíúil.

"Rud éigin cosúil leis sin ach beidh mé i gceart", lig mé gáire mór asam agus mé ag imeacht ón siopa.

Thiomáin mé siar chuig teach Shiobhán ach nuair a baineadh a teach amach, ní raibh mórán spáis ann do mo Juke go dtí go bhfuair mé ceann a bhí leathan go leor os comhair SPAR, in aice le stad bus. Bhí mé ar tí an carr a chúlú nuair a thug mé faoi deara fear ag teacht amach óna teach as eireaball mo shúile. Baineadh geit asam nuair a chonaic mé í sna sála air agus ag tabhairt póige dó.

Chuaigh mé i bhfolach taobh thiar den roth stiúrtha nuair a chuaigh sé trasna na sráide chuig an SPAR, áit a raibh a charr, Qashqai dearg, ach sular léim sé isteach, bhain sé ticéad páirceála dá ghaothscáth agus thosaigh sé ag eascainí. Cá fhad a bhí sé ansin? An raibh sé féin le Siobhán nuair a chuir sí scairt orm ní ba luaithe?

Bhí mé iontach cúramach i dtólamh sa cheantar seo, ag amharc anonn is anall bheith cinnte nach bhfaca duine ar bith mé. Níor thuig mé riamh cén fáth nár thug sí eochair dom, níor strainséir mé tar éis an tsaoil!

Says Himself

Sue Divin

Finally, an early night in my slippers, cradling a cuppa.

Says Himself, 'Mum, you didn't forget my HE homework, did you?'

A vague memory of a request for sweetcorn, ham and chicken pizza topping floats in the fuzz of brain cells from last Tuesday after work... 'Ah...' says me.

'Alexa,' says Himself, 'Set a reminder for 6.45am...'

\#

Himself is itching to cuddle Granny's new dog. For the first time in the two hour journey, he falls quiet as we spy the Armagh spires. Past the mall, the question wriggles out of him. 'Is it a sin to be looking forward to seeing Lucky more than Granny?'

'I think Granny will understand the novelty,' says me.

\#

7.20pm Himself finally settles to homework.

7.22pm 'Mum...?'

Sighing, I don the coat. The maths doled out today is due for tomorrow.

7.40pm B&M bargains. No joy.

7.45pm Tesco metro. Nada.

7.50pm Argos is a long shot but hey. The search suggests my spelling is wrong. Did I mean toy tractors? (They have 7...)

8 pm The first neighbour is apologetic. I am fed up tramping puddles in the dark.

8.10pm Next neighbour reckons maybe but her daughter isn't in until 9...

I hate maths. I was never particularly fond of the borrowing a cup of sugar lark either...

Dear maths teacher,
We do not own a protractor.
Yours sincerely.

#

Friday night TV dinner. Himself and the gadgets plonked across the entire corner sofa. Me in the armchair. Beef chow mein and chicken curry (no onions thank-you). Tastes mighty. Hardly change from Twenty quid but hey, has to be done sometimes.

'What'll we watch?' says me, passing the bag of prawn crackers. We peruse the random list of recordings.

Says Himself, 'How about that Eat Well For Less?'

#

This time, he actually swam. I'm smiling as I pull the car out of the leisure centre car park. He is animated.

'Imagine like if you were the first person ever to swim and you had to work out the physics of it,' says Himself.

I continue driving.

'Like, you couldn't just sit there and expect the water to make you swim and it wouldn't work like speedboats and jet skis with the bubbles coming out the back end...'

#

Says Himself, 'But Mum, the success criteria for the homework says to use adverbs...'

And everything writery in me screams.

He looks up, smiling. 'How about I use strong verbs but *sneakily* squeeze in two adverbs *quietly* to please the teacher?'

#

141

Nothing can knock him off cloud nine today. He is twelve. Everyone in the entire universe must know the significance of this.

6.37am Himself vaults onto my duvet for traditional birthday hugs and reminiscences.

Simple things – ham toastie for breakfast whilst playing Fortnite on new birthday monitor, Snapchat pings from friends.

'Are we really doing McDonald's for lunch?'

'Yes,' says me. 'Have you got your note?'

There is a flourish of crinkled green paper from a pencil case.

12.50pm Chicken selects and fries. I don't even ask if he's apprehensive. He's in awe of the free crunchie McFlurry. He's twelve. It's his day.

2.00pm Appointment. 3 years on NHS waiting lists. 'We can't believe you're here on your birthday,' says one assessor. 'It's great,' says Himself. I'm missing a home-economics test and I don't have to make vegetable soup...'

3.15pm I've explored every app on my phone. He's been in over an hour. Yes, no or more waiting? They call me in while they disappear to confer. 'How'd it go?' I ask. 'Think I did really well,' says Himself, like it was an exam. I wonder...

3.25pm 'Ms Divin?' I'm ushered in for the pronouncement. 'We'll leave it the parent to explain to the child,' they say. I smile, relieved.

3.40pm Barely out the door into wind and rain. Himself is itching to know.

'They said yes. For definite. And how amazing you are to cope with so much.'

A passing car scoots a tidal wave from a puddle and we're drenched on the pavement. Himself laughs. 'I thought that only happened in the movies! It's like everything on my birthday is magic.'

'So, how do you feel?' I ask.

'About being diagnosed with autism?' His hair drips. He smiles the biggest most amazing twelve-year-old smile. 'Sure I'll always be me, no matter what.'

Nothing can knock him off cloud nine today. He is twelve. Everyone in the entire universe must know the significance of this.

Reading the Trees

Damien Mallon

For Tony Crozier

You couldn't know but now
You are reading the trees,
The ones from Carnagh woods
They were felled late last autumn,
That whole green hillside's now a-stubble
Grabbed up in twig-like bundles
To be mulched into paper.
But I remember when summer rainbows
Foretold of westerly rain showers in arches
Over your emerald peaked canopy
I sheltered under this very one.
Touched the bluebell's bells
Watched an ant climb a trumpet mushroom.
I kissed a girl against that one.
She wore a summer cotton print dress
I picked the bark-moss off her back
As we walked on together through the trees,
In the autumn ferns under those two
Planted too closely together,
A wounded cock pheasant sheltered
'Till a busy spaniel took him to hand.
In here the soldiers sheltered
Men with woolly faces conspired
Wood pigeons flighted to dusky roosts
And the big tawny owl hoot-hooted.
The trees would rather we remembered them alive

In the musty smell of forest floor
In the stickiness of their amber sap
In these few lines written on their skin

Previously Published in *Reading the Trees* by Damien Mallon.

The Joke

Csilla Toldy

We came from a mould of cruelty after the war. As children, we were beaten at school, as adults, we were taken from trains and thrown into nothingness. As losers of the war, abused by the winners, given nothing, our wives mass-raped to humiliate us. They called themselves our liberators and we had to pretend that we loved and saw them as our big friend, all a pretence. Then again, Hungarians killed Hungarians. Religion did not matter any more. You could only survive with jokes.

'What's the tragedy of the Twentieth Century?'

'That the Titanic sank and not the Aurora.'

The Russians thought we were all Nazis, which was not true. We just did what we were told to do; as good Christians went to church.

My wife is very religious, but now that has to be kept a secret, too. Margit plays the piano at no end. The children are hungry, she would rather starve, but she wouldn't sell the piano. Sometimes I think, she is mad. Strauss, Schubert - she loves to sing, too. Oh, that wonderful voice, like an opera singer, never broken. Shall I tell you another joke?

'President Rákosi personally wants to check his own popularity among his people. Incognito, he enters a cinema and soon, he sees his own self proudly presented in the prequel news. The whole cinema audience stands up in ovation, while he sits contented in his chair when someone taps his bald head from behind:

"Stand up and clap your hands, little baldie, before the secret police takes you!"'

I was drunk when they took me off the tram. Just said a joke about Rákosi, a joke about him outside Heaven's Gate. The trip was still a drunken stupor, but soon I was no longer drunk, the pain sobered me up and made me pray and pray while being beaten. The

145

walls were cold - no heating, no paint. I was in a cellar. I knew that there was a world outside, but nobody could hear me shouting. My voice non-existent, my life worthless in the eyes of people that have no compassion, following orders blindly, directed and manipulated by fear and the inherent cruelty.

Why did I drink? Dear God, why did I drink? Margit told me not to. It made me bold, she said, and then I talked too much. I was begging them through my broken teeth, spitting blood:

'It was just a joke, please, it was just a joke.'

Dried blood covers the walls. This has been the last station for so many a men before me. My body will never be found, it will disappear down the drains, into the river. Into the Blue Danube, dear God, save me from fear.

The Joke by Csilla Toldy first appeared in *The Emigrant Woman's Tale* Lapwing Publications (2015) ISBN 978-1909252998 [book and CD]

A Fond Farewell

Karen Mooney

Stand easy Dad, this shift is over;
salute, left turn, fall out
Now the time has come for another role.
Let there be no doubt
that your gentle squeeze of my hand
offered to comfort you, in your own way,
reassured to spell the future out.

Not a man of words for family
yet speeches never fazed;
formality, authority, a presence
that left many so amazed
with signals, a stance, a look;
sometimes a furrowed brow.

Commanding our attention, even in death,
you somehow summoned the strength
to say everything; no words got in the way.
Piercing looks, intense; a smile;
over another's shoulder, a wink;
that mischief ever present,
knowing exactly what I would think.

Once a bear of a man, such stature;
physical strength now leached by death.
Yet, the character remains; honed,
even mellowed with each lessening breath.

A lifetime of avoiding intimacy
yet you seemed to crave my touch; or,
perhaps knowing that I needed yours;
that I was just being brave.

That promised final drink
Well, I closed the door,
placed that stout soaked sponge to your lips,
saluted you with the tin then raised it to my own.
The look on your face was priceless
as you sucked that sponge like a child;
eyes gleaming, smiling,
a temporary release from a living hell.

Knowing that you were going 'home,'
blind eyes were turned, no-one would tell.
But word got out; staff, cheered internally
at our final act of defiance: you raised me well.

We talked, well I did; you listened.
Covered all the bases and you,
content that all would be well,
turned your mind to other places.

Restful, peaceful,
stepping back from duty
yet still wilfully displaying
that even in death there's beauty.

ABOUT THE EDITORS

Réamonn Ó Ciaráin has spent more than twenty years working with Gael Linn in the promotion of the Irish language. He has a special interest in the stories of the Ulster Cycle since childhood. Réamonn was born in Crossmaglen and now lives in Milford near Navan Fort. After leaving the Abbey Grammar School in Newry, he completed a degree in education with celtic studies at St. Mary's University College, Belfast. Following this Réamonn successfully completed postgraduate studies in Queen's University Belfast and then at University of Ulster, Jordanstown. Réamonn is closely involved in the monthly production of An tUltach, Ireland's oldest literary magazine and became chairman of its board of directors in 2010. Réamonn is a director of The Cardinal Ó Fiaich Library and Archives. He has held the position of Public Relations Officer with Armagh County Board of the GAA, Irish Language Officer for County Armagh, Children's Officer for County Armagh and is a member of the GAA's national committee for the Irish language. Réamonn is an active member of Cairde Teo and Aonach Mhacha in Armagh City.

His publications include:
Laoch na Laochra - Scéal Chúchulainn published by Gael Linn, 2015
Cúchulainn, Ulster's Greatest Hero published by Gael Linn, 2017
Cú Uladh - Scéal Chúchulainn published by Gael Linn, 2018

Byddi Lee grew up in Armagh and moved to Belfast to study at Queen's University. She has since lived in South Africa, Canada, California and Paris before returning to live in her hometown, Armagh. She has published flash fiction, short stories and self-published her novel, *March to November* in 2014. Byddi also writes a blog about life, both at home and abroad called, *We didn't come here for the grass*. She co-runs Flash Fiction Armagh and volunteers as a board member for the John O Connor Writing School in Armagh. She currently is writing a trilogy set in a near future Ireland.